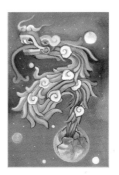

THE TOLTEC
I CHING

THE
TOLTEC
I CHING

64 KEYS TO INSPIRED ACTION
IN THE NEW WORLD

Martha Ramirez-Oropeza

William Douglas Horden

Larson Publications

BURDETT, NEW YORK

ISBN 13: 978-0-943914-99-2
ISBN 10: 0-943914-99-X

Library of Congress Control Number: 2008944389

Publisher's Cataloging-In-Publication Data
(Prepared by The Donohue Group, Inc.)

Ramirez-Oropeza, Martha.
   The Toltec I ching : 64 keys to inspired action in the new world / Martha
Ramirez-Oropeza [and] William Douglas Horden.

   p. : col. ill. ; cm.

   Includes index.
   ISBN-13: 978-0-943914-99-2
   ISBN-10: 0-943914-99-X

   1. Yi jing. 2. Toltec philosophy. 3. Conduct of life. I. Horden, William
Douglas. II. Title.

PL2464.Z7 R36 2009
299.5/1282   2008944389

Printed in China by Everbest Printing Company through
Four Colour Print Group in Louisville, Kentucky

Published by Larson Publications
4936 NYS Route 414
Burdett, New York 14818 USA
www.larsonpublications.com

18   17   16   15   14   13   12   11   10   09
10   9   8   7   6   5   4   3   2   1

CONTENTS

LIST OF TABLES

INTRODUCTION

The Eternal Path

Although the outer world has changed dramatically in the past several thousand years, the inner world of the soul remains unchanged since the time of the ancients. The inner life of our ancestors, particularly the soul questions and soul decisions they faced, was no different than our own:

What is my purpose in life?

Why must all that I know and love die?

Is there a meaning to this universe I find myself in?

In all the known world, why are human beings the only ones with doubt?

How can I be sure of the right thing to do?

How can I eradicate wrong without doing wrong?

What is real success, real progress, real power?

Is my fate predetermined or am I creating the person I choose to be?

How can I face my own death with calm joy and an unshakeable sense of victory?

What is the best path of life and how do I keep from stepping off it?

The inner path each of us takes is determined by the way we answer soul questions and act on soul decisions. While it takes great courage to not fall in line with the forces of materialism and self-interest, it requires even greater courage to hold to our path for an entire lifetime. It is in the nature of people to rebel against the prevailing view when they are young or passing through unexpected trials, but too few use those opportunities to take up a way of life that will last them forever. The longing for recognition, acceptance, and approval drives most of us to pursue the external goals of those around us. For this reason, difficult as it is to step onto the spiritual path, it is many times more difficult to finish the journey still on the path.

How to bring the inner and outer worlds into balance and harmony so that we might live a vital and meaningful life—*that* is the soul question whose answer places us firmly on the lifelong path of spiritual transformation, evolution, and metamorphosis. How to bring our inner intent and outer actions into balance and harmony so that we might contribute to others living vital and meaningful lives—*that* is the soul decision whose implementation keeps us from stepping onto the path of materialism, self-interest, and spiritual stagnation.

The more complex and divisive the outer world becomes, the more difficult it is to find the harmony and balance between it and the inner world of the soul. Competing interests and ideologies vie for our energy and devotion, factions of every type call us to join their side. Technology continually threatens to change the way we interact with one another and nature. The pendulum of history continues to swing between those who control resources and those who will control them. The generations pass and old animosities become dominant landmarks of civilization instead of deserted ruins in a long-forgotten past. Advancements that promise peace and prosperity for all seem instead to end up serving the interests of those who benefit from conflict and inequality. We come into this world with an innate sense of rightness and find ourselves instructed from all sides to replace it with a form of practicality that keeps the mistakes of the past alive. Every generation, we find it more difficult to withstand the demand for conformity—and even more difficult to permanently change our surroundings for the better. When the outer world is so far out of balance and harmony with itself, how are we to find balance and harmony between it and the inner world of the soul?

There are two ways to approach this problem. The first is by adopting a new global perspective. It entails viewing this period in history as a time of transition between the Old World of conflict and greed and the New World of peace and prospering for all. It involves not naive idealism but, rather, the most even-handed pragmatism. Only naive ideologues believe that civilization can continue on its present course—every practical person in the world can see that civilization must undergo a profound metamorphosis if it is to avoid certain self-destruction. We have reached a time when everyone has access to all the information they need to reach this conclusion. Because those in positions of power are loath to abandon their Old World dreams of conquest and domination, it falls to the rest of us to bring about the reality of the New World of harmony between humanity, nature, and the sacred. Never have so many been so well-informed. Or well-intentioned. Or inspired. It is no exaggeration to say that all of human history has been leading up to this time in which we can reshape our common destiny.

The movement away from the Old World of force and competition toward the New World of ethics and cooperation, then, is a natural metamorphosis of the baser instincts into the higher aspirations. Toward this end, *The Toltec I Ching* sets out a practical code of conduct and perception that has been long held by the savants of every culture to assure the founding of the Golden Age of Humanity.

The second approach is by adopting a new individual perspective. It entails trying to see through the complexity of our surroundings and into the essential relationships we have with the outer world—by trying, in other words, to concentrate less on understanding our surroundings and more on understanding our responses to what is happening around us. By focusing on our responses instead of our circumstances, we are able to develop a consistent strategy of behavior that is based on values and integrity instead of guesswork and mind reading. Because the complex and ever-changing nature of the outer world makes it impossible to ever have enough information to make a decision with absolute certainty, it is best to return to the unchanging inner world of the soul for a map of time-proven responses that chart the course of a successful life.

Long before the outer world reached its present level of complexity, the ancients explored the inner world of the soul in order to conceive a map of orderly responses human beings might make to the chaos of circumstances faced in the course of a lifetime. This is an eminently practical approach because experience teaches that even though we have little control of the circumstances we face in life, we have the potential for complete control of our responses to them. It is this move—away from trying to control the world and toward trying to control our responses to it—that can be said to mark the starting point of the ancients' wisdom.

Until we as individuals achieve some mastery of our responses to events, in other words, we have little hope of fulfilling our ancestors' vision of an uninterrupted reign of peace and prosperity for all. Although the question of what it is that we are collectively building may seem far removed from our daily concerns and activities, experience teaches that our intention to achieve a goal is what gets us to the goal. Just as the wind arrives ahead of the rain, our intention to create peace and prosperity for all is the necessary precursor to reaching that most ancient of goals.

Of more immediate concern, of course, is the capacity each of us possesses for achieving a sense of well-being, happiness, and success in life regardless of the twists and turns of fate we encounter. Here, too, it is our inner responses that determine how we interpret, how we feel about, and how we react to the circumstances with which we are presented. Again, it is when we stop trying to control how others are treating us and begin trying to control how we are treating others that we can be said to be putting the ancients' wisdom into practice. By setting aside hopes and disappointments and concentrating instead on integrity and consistency, we can move beyond the cycle of desire and frustration into the cycle of authenticity and fulfillment.

In this sense, we are seeking to control our outer responses by first controlling our inner responses. It is clearly impossible to make long-lasting changes in our behavior until we have changed the thoughts and feelings that make us behave as we do. While we were trained by those around us to think and feel in certain ways that have become inner habits, however, the training to replace those habits with new, more authentic, habits has to be done on our own. This takes time and will power. It takes dedication and passion. It takes sincerity and seriousness of purpose. It takes the kind of courage that is able to face self-defeating behaviors and patiently, persistently, overcome them. It takes the kind of training that puts a time-honored code of conduct and perception into daily practice.

When someone works like this at self-transformation they are said to be a spirit warrior.

The Spirit Warrior

It has long been observed that people can be overcome without force if their spirit can be defeated first. The opposite, of course, is equally true: Even when defeated by force, people cannot be overcome so long as their spirit remains undefeated.

When we think of being overcome, we think first about threats to our personal freedom and safety. Being overcome, after all, can occur in various ways: physically, economically, culturally, psychologically. And the dynamics of being overcome, moreover, can involve different numbers of people: An individual can be overcome by another individual, an individual can be overcome by a group, a group can be overcome by an individual, and a group can be overcome by another group. Personal experience and the lessons of history can provide each of us with examples of all these forms of either being overcome or of overcoming others.

While it may be a little more difficult, we can also find examples in which the effort to overcome was thwarted by a spirit so indomitable it could not be defeated. Such examples provide us with a picture of the spirit warrior's actions in the outer world but they do not necessarily open a window onto the ongoing war the spirit warrior wages on the battlefield of the inner world of the soul. This difference is important because the capacity to resist being overcome in the outer world is a direct reflection of our capacity to resist being overcome by our inner fears, doubts, and passions. It is here, on this inner battlefield, that we confront the perennial enemy, the real enemy, the most insidious enemy. It is here, in the daily war within the inner world of the soul, that we confront the enemy-within, that shadow side of ourselves making up all our self-defeating attitudes and behaviors.

This is the real and consequential war we each face because the indomitable spirit that cannot be overcome in the outer world does not arise from a person suffering daily defeat from within. For this reason, spirit warriors are not defined by their battles in the outer world—rather, they are defined by their conscientious dedication to defeating the enemy-within.

Our self-defeating attitudes and behaviors continue even when we wish them to stop because they have become habits of thought, feeling, and memory. To defeat our self-defeating habits, it is necessary to replace them with new and decisively constructive habits of thought, feeling, and memory. The training this requires involves no less effort than that of an athlete or a musician to reach the pinnacle of their respective accomplishments. There are some important differences, however. Whereas athletes and musicians generally display some special talent or interest before they are seriously trained in their fields, every one of us has the innate capacity to be a spirit warrior—all we need is the sincere desire to defeat our self-defeating behaviors so that we might discover our true self and our true potential. Likewise, whereas athletes and musicians begin by training their outer actions first and their inner actions second, spirit warriors begin by training their inner actions first and their outer actions second—we work to gain control of our outer responses by first gaining control of our inner responses.

Such training means finding a new way to look at the world and then consistently acting internally in harmony with that vision— allowing our thoughts and feelings to be shaped by our vision of the world rather than by those whose vision may be based on a world view that is essentially materialistic and self-serving. As unintentional a consequence as it may be, adopting a world view that holds all of creation to be spiritual and its purpose worth serving inevitably results in our vision of the world more closely resembling that of the ancients than that of our contemporaries.

For this reason, we return to the lessons the ancients distilled from their vision of the world: The whole of the spirit warrior's training consists of learning to treat the world as a living spirit of infinite form and then to translate the ancients' lessons into a way of life that proves meaningful and effective today.

The Toltec I Ching

We keep alive the ancient way of life when we view matter and spirit as two halves of our world. We disrupt that continuity, on the other hand, in those moments when we see nature as something separate from ourselves, or view the physical world as not spiritual, or perceive matter as dead and not miraculous. We keep the old ways alive by experiencing nature as the visible, external half of spirit—and spirit as the invisible, internal half of nature. This is an experience that touches us on the personal level when we see our body as the visible, external half of our spirit and our spirit as the invisible, internal half of our body.

Such a vision permits us to reach the unitary nature of the world lying just beyond the barrier of our senses. One of the principal consequences of this way of looking at the world is a belief in the invisible interconnectedness of all things. From such a perspective, the connections between things express the laws of spiritual cause-and-effect which, although not always within the grasp of our understanding, give our lives meaning, purpose, and a sense of direction. These connections, furthermore, express the general flow, or direction, of the world at large and, as such, communicate to us the best course to follow at any given time. Where these communications are recognized in the course of everyday life, they are called intuitions or omens. Where they have been worked into a consistent and comprehensive system of interpretation, they are called oracles or divination.

While the world view that gives rise to divination can be found in many ancient cultures of the world, it is in those of ancient Asia and the Americas that divinatory systems are especially well developed. This is particularly the case with the *I Ching (Book of Changes)*[1] of ancient China and the *Tonalpoalli (Sacred Calendar)* of ancient Mexico.[2] Similarities between these ancient cultures are not coincidental, of course, as they share a common ancestry in the mother culture that existed before people crossed between Asia and the Americas.

Despite the differences time and distance wrought between those ancient cultures as they developed over the millennia, numerous similarities persisted that hint at the world view of their common ancestors.³ Building on these similarities, *The Toltec I Ching* combines the lessons of the traditional *I Ching* and the *Tonalpoalli* into a modern expression of those ancient oracles. Toward this end, each of the 64 hexagrams of the *I Ching* have been translated into an Illustration whose images reflect the continuity of the ancient culture that is still a vital part of the way of life in modern-day Mexico and northern Central America.

The Illustrations here are inspired both by the ancient and contemporary, combining the symbolism of the ancient Toltec pictorial writing system with that of the modern muralist tradition. The written material here interprets the symbolism of each hexagram, incorporating the lessons of the *I Ching* and the *Tonalpoalli* into descriptions of those actions and intentions which represent the most balanced and harmonious responses to events. In this sense, *The Toltec I Ching* is the latest incarnation of the ancient Oracle which, in some long-distant past, provided the inspiration for both the *I Ching* and the *Tonalpoalli.*

A New Arrangement of the I Ching Hexagrams

The Toltec I Ching marks a radical departure from the traditional arrangement of the 64 situations, or *hexagrams,* as they are called. That traditional arrangement of the hexagrams is often referred to as the King Wen sequence, named for the patriarch of the Chou Dynasty (1150–249 B.C.). That sequence of the 64 hexagrams forms the basis of what has come to be thought of as the *I Ching,* or *Book of Changes.* Its formal name, however, is the *Chou I,* or *Changes of Chou,* commemorating the fact that the Oracle was reconceived from an earlier one belonging to the Shang Dynasty.⁴ It is this *Chou I,* then, that we have come to identify with the *I Ching.*

But this arrangement of the hexagrams into the King Wen Sequence is not the only order into which the hexagrams have historically been placed. At least two earlier versions of the *I Ching* existed, one from the Shang Dynasty (1766–1150 B.C.) and another from the Hsia Dynasty (2205–1766 B.C.)—and both these earlier versions arranged the 64 hexa-

grams in an order different than the surviving King Wen sequence.[5]
It is not only their arrangements of the hexagrams that distinguished
these earlier versions from the *Chou I:* Consisting of little more than
the hexagrams and their names, they lacked the written interpretive
commentary that was added in the later Chou version.[6]

Moreover, the discovery in 1973 of the oldest existing copy of the
I Ching at Mawangdui, dated to about 190 B.C., places the 64 hexagrams in a completely different arrangement than that in the King
Wen sequence—and calls many of the hexagrams by names different than those in the traditional *I Ching.*[7] Although the Mawangdui
manuscript is the oldest copy of the *I Ching,* it is almost certainly of
a later date than the traditional King Wen version[8] and demonstrates
that neither the order of the hexagrams nor their names were ever to
be treated as the sole and permanent expressions of the Oracle.

Historically, therefore, the core of the *I Ching* has been viewed as a
system of 64 symbols the arrangement and interpretation of which are
both open to change. Indeed, the concept of the *Book of Changes* as a
static and monolithic text is antithetical to the world view of constant
change that it espouses. This is not simply conjecture, however: The
fact that each of three succeeding dynasties possessed their own version of the *I Ching* demonstrates that the arrangement and meaning
of the hexagrams coincided with real-world changes in the current of
human history. Far from being an anachronistic relic relevant only
to times past, in other words, the *I Ching* originally was viewed as a
timeless structure that had to be periodically revised in order to reinvigorate its meaning in contemporary life.

The order of the hexagrams as they relate to *The Toltec I Ching* represents just such a modern revision of the King Wen sequence of the
Chou I. Certainly there are many factors that can be cited to justify
such a revision but all of them pale beside this: The *Chou I* was written
to educate rulers in the hope of providing an enlightened leadership
capable of bringing lasting benefit to its people. After three thousand
years of experience, it can safely be said that noble effort has failed
and that, to the contrary, we already have entered a new "dynasty" of
history—one in which the goals of power and the tools of enforce-

ment increasingly turn to controlling society rather than benefiting it. It is for this reason that an underlying theme of *The Toltec I Ching* addresses the strategies by which individuals might thrive in the midst of injustice without becoming unjust and, ultimately, effect changes that establish a "dynasty" in which the promise of humanity living in harmony with nature, spirit, and itself is fulfilled.

The Organization of the Hexagrams

Each hexagram represents a situation that is part of the entire world view of 64 situations. The meaning of each hexagram, therefore, makes up one part of the overall meaning of the entire system of 64 hexagrams. By changing the order in which the hexagrams are arranged, their part in the Oracle as a whole changes. By changing the relationships between the hexagrams in this way, their relative meanings change. These new meanings are reflected in the written interpretations and their accompanying illustrations, which together give voice to this modern revision of the ancient Oracle.

The actual sequence of *The Toltec I Ching* arrangement of the hexagrams is based on that of the traditional King Wen sequence through a process of trigram substitution.

Because those familiar with the *I Ching* are accustomed to working with the hexagrams in the traditional King Wen sequence, the chart below is provided as a tool for transposing between the two sequences. Either sequence (Toltec or King Wen) can be assigned to column A, and column B will show the corresponding hexagram in the other sequence.

It is a peculiar characteristic of this table that a hexagram number from either sequence located in Column A will show the hexagram number from the corresponding sequence in Column B. In other words: Hexagram 1 in the Toltec sequence corresponds to Hexagram 51 in the King Wen sequence *and* Hexagram 1 in the King Wen sequence corresponds to Hexagram 51 in the Toltec sequence, Hexagram 2 in the Toltec sequence corresponds to Hexagram 58 in the King Wen *and* Hexagram 2 of King Wen corresponds to Hexagram 58 of the Toltec, and so on.

Table 1: Transposing between the Toltec and King Wen sequences

A	B	A	B	A	B	A	B
1	51	17	11	33	55	49	15
2	58	18	64	34	25	50	4
3	9	19	45	35	41	51	1
4	50	20	60	36	31	52	30
5	42	21	26	37	39	53	63
6	32	22	56	38	23	54	12
7	28	23	38	39	37	55	33
8	61	24	43	40	44	56	22
9	3	25	34	41	35	57	29
10	16	26	21	42	5	58	2
11	17	27	14	43	24	59	48
12	54	28	7	44	40	60	20
13	62	29	57	45	19	61	8
14	27	30	52	46	47	62	13
15	49	31	36	47	46	63	53
16	10	32	6	48	59	64	18

Studying the Cycle of Metamorphosis

The 64 hexagrams make up a cycle of the dynamics of metamorphosis, which can be studied as a whole to gain a perspective on situations beyond our own immediate concerns. Such a perspective allows us to understand the root causes of problems and their prospective remedies—which, in turn, allows us to be of greater benefit to all our lives touch. By following the progression of metamorphosis as it moves from the first hexagram to the last—and then starts over with the first in order to repeat the cycle—we come to a better understanding of the ever-changing cycles of action-and-backlash governing the waxing and waning of fortune.

The principal reason for studying the sequence of 64 situations is to be able to recognize the factors driving events and then fashion responses that make the most of present opportunities. Avoiding difficulties that can be avoided, surviving difficulties that cannot be avoided, passing up opportunities that lead in the wrong direction, creating future successes by making them inevitable in the present: Such are the adaptations we make to the wide range of circumstances we face in life. But good decisions alone are not enough to fashion a meaningful life—it is also necessary to carry the right intention at all times. Things happen unexpectedly and take us by surprise. If we are not mentally and emotionally prepared ahead of time, we are caught off-guard and make mistakes that come back to haunt us later. If we are concerned only with material benefit and our own self-interest, then it is by our intention that we cause our own downfall. This is no less true of organizations and nations than it is of individuals and small groups of people.

Because the dynamics of change apply equally to the individual and the collective, the cycle of 64 phases of metamorphosis can be studied in a historical context, particularly in terms of rectifying past relationships and improving the outlook for the future. By identifying where in the cycle of 64 phases an entity—whether a group or an individual—stands, it becomes possible to predict the obstacles and opportunities ahead. Such foresight allows us to plan with confidence in our ability to adapt to the future and effect a strategy that benefits the greatest number.

In this sense, the cycle of metamorphosis is cosmological—that is, it reflects the dynamics of creation and change that guide the development of all entities at every level, from the course of the universe itself to the life of the individual. This mirroring of the macrocosmic and microcosmic worlds is a direct manifestation of the unitary nature of existence, which is everywhere guided from within by the interaction of the masculine and feminine creative forces. Indeed, the way in which the Oracle communicates with human beings—through the hexagrams—is wholly the symbolic representation of the 64 possible ways that the masculine and feminine forces take turns occupying the six archetypal levels, or lines, of the divinatory moment.

Study of this grand cycle of metamorphosis generally begins with the first two hexagrams— "Provoking Change" and "Sensing Creation," respectively—as they constitute the parent forces, so to speak, from which all the other 62 hexagrams develop. After considering how these two primal forces unite to produce all subsequent change, the remaining 31 pairs of hexagrams can be seen to unfold in the natural course of action-reaction.

Studying the Cycle of Metamorphosis like this is traditionally seen as using the *I Ching* as a book of wisdom, of counsel, by which we train ourselves to perceive the essence of situations and respond in a way that increases our adaptability and sense of well-being. As we familiarize ourselves with the 64 hexagrams as a whole, we increasingly come to express the principle of metamorphosis in our daily lives. Since most of our habits of thought and emotion were instilled in us by our social and physical surroundings long before we were capable of giving our consent, it is only right and fitting that we take up that training consciously once we determine that the old habits are holding us back from reaching our full potential.

Over the course of time, we come to embody the Cycle of Metamorphosis and give its perennial truth a new individual form in the historical epoch in which we live.

How to Consult the Oracle

An Oracle is a system of symbols that allows the One Spirit to communicate with human beings. Most ancient peoples viewed the world as spirit, no less alive and aware in nature than in human nature—a world view many modern people are finding best expresses their own personal experience of life.

As the eternal home from which all spirits or souls come and to which they all return, the One Spirit is the treasury of all the memories and experiences of all who have ever lived. More than that, however, as the creator and sustainer of all that exists, the One Spirit has its own purpose and intention, its own goal and means of achieving that goal.

The lessons derived from both the ancient Toltec and Chinese world views clearly demonstrate that the One Spirit seeks an ennobling of the human spirit that brings peace and prospering to all. This goal is often thought of as the *universal civilizing spirit*, an invisible but somehow tangible drive from within to transcend the animal instincts and create a just and humane New World for all. The means to achieving this goal, however, is not pictured as some set of fixed values that can be commanded from on high. Rather, it is seen as depending on the metamorphosis of the individual. The Oracle, in other words, teaches us to be more adaptable and happier in the face of inevitable change because individuals who do so will create the New World out of the ashes of the old.

In consulting the Oracle, then, it is useful to keep these ideas in mind, which might be summarized as: *I am part of the Living Whole that wants the best for me and all others at the same time.*

In interpreting the Oracle's response, it is helpful to recall that it is describing the *essence* of situations, not the specific external events. It is expressing the laws of spiritual cause-and-effect, which operate everywhere from within, so its answer describes the inner state of the situation and, especially, the most appropriate way to respond to the situation.

In understanding the mechanism by which the Oracle works, moreover, it is useful to contemplate the unitary nature of spirit and matter while sensing how the One Spirit expresses itself by altering the 50-50 probability of one side over the other in the random falling of coins. Because our thoughts are part of the One Spirit, which is itself the immaterial half of the material world, the Oracle is able to answer us by tipping the scales of chance in favor of meaningful coincidence.

So, first and foremost, engage the Oracle with sincerity and an openness to learn—not just to learn how to survive change, but with a willingness to change along with change. Set aside any convictions about cause-and-effect for the time being and try to sense the immediate interconnectedness of all things.

Second, focus on the subject of your inquiry. What are you really trying to understand? Try to get to a feeling level, sensing the inner motivation for asking. Avoid the temptation to be too specific or to focus on just one question. Try writing down a number of questions that cluster around your focus, especially if you ask from slightly different viewpoints. For example:

How should I respond to this deteriorating relationship?

Is it possible to salvage it?

How should I treat the other person?

Are there mistakes I ought to try to correct?

Is my present course of conduct leading me where I wish to go?

Third, with your set of related questions written on the same sheet of paper, consult the Oracle using the coin method described in detail in the next section "Casting and Interpreting the Oracle." Follow those directions, writing down the Hexagram Numbers and their Line Changes.

Fourth, consider the Oracle's answer in light of your questions. Begin by reflecting on the Illustration and the description of its Image and Interpretation, using it as a mirror of your inner process. This part of the reading speaks most directly to your unconscious, symbol-making self. Then move on to the text for Action and Intent, observing what direction the Oracle advises you to take and with what purpose in mind. This part of the reading speaks to the general context of the situation and, most especially, the kind of mental and emotional response appropriate to the time. Lastly, move on to the Summary, which is the most concise part of the reading and speaks directly to your most conscious self.

The Oracle's answer is generally clear; but if it is not immediately so, delay forming an opinion. Give yourself a few days to reflect on it. It is often the case that the Oracle seems to answer a question that we did not ask—or answers it from a larger context than we were seeing at the time. This happens, of course, because the Oracle gives voice to the One Spirit, which is aware of our deeper needs and responds to them as if asked. Since the Oracle is describing the essence of situations from the broadest of contexts, it may not always be immediately clear which parts relate to you and which relate to others. For this reason, it is best to re-read its answer a day or two later, letting its initial impact sink in.

Fifth, keep in mind that the Oracle is describing the archetypal patterns of change and their trends. They are relatively easy to discern in the movement of the Present Hexagram to the Future Hexagram evolving out of it. Patterns of change and trends can be a little more difficult to discern immediately in the readings of the Line Changes.

This is because the Line Changes mark the *transitions* between the Present and Future Hexagrams. Like landmarks, they can sometimes be a little difficult to see ahead of time. I might know I ought to take the right fork in the road by the ruins of a castle, but I cannot do more than imagine it until I actually arrive. And it may look entirely different than I imagined. But I recognize it when I get there.

Sixth, in interpreting the Line Changes it is useful to see them as occurring in the order they are cast. In other words, in those readings with more than one Line Change, the transitions to the Future Hexagram will occur in the order they are thrown—from bottom to top. If the 2ND, 4TH, and 5TH lines were to change, for example, then the transition expressed in the 2nd line would occur before the 4TH, just as that expressed by the 4TH would occur before that of the 5TH.

It can also be useful to keep in mind that the six lines of each Hexagram signify the six archetypal stages of development within a situation. These can be expressed by the essential *issues* they represent:

6TH   DISENGAGEMENT

5TH   AUTHORITY

4TH   RESPONSIBILITY

3RD   ALIENATION

2ND   TRUST

1ST   DEPENDENCE

When the Oracle answers with Line Changes in the 2ND, 4TH, and 5TH stages, for example, the *issue* of Trust may refer to you or to others, the *issue* of Responsibility may refer to you or to others, the *issue* of Authority may refer to you or to others.

While it is not necessary to consider the Line Changes in this detail, in some circumstances it may help clarify the underlying, essential, nature of the transitions-at-hand.

And, lastly, it can be especially helpful to keep a journal with the dates of your questions and the Oracle's answers recorded so you can go back and see how the course of events unfolded.

CASTING AND INTERPRETING THE ORACLE

There are various methods of consulting the *I Ching* oracle, but the most popular is the coin oracle. What follows is the standard way to cast an *I Ching* oracle using coins.

Step One: Preparation

- Locate three coins of the same denomination.
- Assign the value "3" to heads and "2" to tails.
- Have paper and pen or pencil at hand.
- Until you become familiar with the method, begin by creating the following chart.

6TH THROW	_____	= _____
5TH THROW	_____	= _____
4TH THROW	_____	= _____
3RD THROW	_____	= _____
2ND THROW	_____	= _____
1ST THROW	_____	= _____

Step Two: Casting the Oracle

1. Either formulate a question or ask for a reflection of yourself at this time.
2. Shake the coins between your hands until it feels right to toss them in front of you.
3. Jot down a "3" for each heads and a "2" for each tails.
4. Repeat this process five times until you have made a total of six throws.

5. Since the results of the six throws are numbered vertically, record the *first throw at the bottom line* and the *sixth throw at the top line*, as in the example below.

EXAMPLE

6TH THROW	3 + 3 + 2 = ____
5TH THROW	2 + 2 + 2 = ____
4TH THROW	3 + 2 + 2 = ____
3RD THROW	3 + 3 + 2 = ____
2ND THROW	3 + 2 + 2 = ____
1ST THROW	3 + 3 + 3 = ____

6. After completing the sixth throw, set aside the coins and total up the values of each throw.

EXAMPLE

6TH THROW	3 + 3 + 2 = 8
5TH THROW	2 + 2 + 2 = 6
4TH THROW	3 + 2 + 2 = 7
3RD THROW	3 + 3 + 2 = 8
2ND THROW	3 + 2 + 2 = 7
1ST THROW	3 + 3 + 3 = 9

7. Next to each of these totals, place the corresponding line:

6	—— x ——	(CHANGING YIN LINE)
7	————	(STABLE YANG LINE)
8	—— ——	(STABLE YIN LINE)
9	——o——	(CHANGING YANG LINE)

By converting the numerical values of the six throws into their corresponding lined figures, we are able to construct the six-lined "hexagrams" that symbolize the 64 answers of the I Ching oracle.

8. Following our example, this conversion constructs the first hexagram of the reading.

EXAMPLE

6TH THROW	3 + 3 + 2 = 8	—— ——
5TH THROW	2 + 2 + 2 = 6	—— x ——
4TH THROW	3 + 2 + 2 = 7	————
3RD THROW	3 + 3 + 2 = 8	—— ——
2ND THROW	3 + 2 + 2 = 7	————
1ST THROW	3 + 3 + 3 = 9	——o——

The lined figures corresponding to "6" and "9" represent the so-called "changing lines" of the I Ching, and need to be resolved into "7s" and "8s".

9. If there are any *6s* or *9s* in your hexagram, then make a copy of the hexagram to the right, replacing the lined figure of each *6* with that of a *7* and the lined figure of each *9* with that of an *8* (from step 7, above).

EXAMPLE	6TH	8	— —	— —
	5TH	6	— x —	————
	4TH	7	————	————
	3RD	8	— —	— —
	2ND	7	————	————
	1ST	9	—o—	— —

Note that the second hexagram is constructed by copying any "7" or "8" just as they are, and changing only the "6s" and "9s" into their opposites.

- This concludes the process of casting the Oracle.
- The next step is to identify the hexagrams in the Oracle's answer and refer to their respective interpretive texts.

Step Three: Interpreting the Oracle's Answer

To begin with, it is necessary to note that each *hexagram* is composed of two *trigrams*—the *lower trigram* being made up of the bottom three lines (1ST, 2ND, 3RD) of the hexagram and the *upper trigram* being made up of the top three lines (4TH, 5TH, 6TH) of the hexagram.

Following the example from above, the two hexagrams can be divided into their respective trigrams.

EXAMPLE	LINE		FIRST HEXAGRAM	→	SECOND HEXAGRAM	
	6TH	8	— —	→	— —	
	5TH	6	— x —	→	————	UPPER TRIGRAM
	4TH	7	————	→	————	
	3RD	8	— —	→	— —	
	2ND	7	————	→	————	LOWER TRIGRAM
	1ST	9	—o—	→	— —	

Table 2: Chart of Trigrams and Hexagrams

	Upper Trigram							
	☰	☱	☲	☳	☴	☵	☶	☷
Lower Trigram (☰)	2	23	8	45	16	12	20	35
(☱)	15	52	39	31	62	33	53	56
(☲)	7	4	29	47	40	6	59	64
(☳)	19	41	60	58	54	10	61	38
(☴)	24	27	3	17	51	25	42	21
(☵)	11	26	5	43	34	1	9	14
(☶)	46	18	48	28	32	44	57	50
(☷)	36	22	63	49	55	13	37	30

Locate your hexagram number at the point where its upper and lower trigrams intersect.

1. Use the Chart of Trigrams and Hexagrams above to locate the *trigrams* making up the first *hexagram* of your reading.

2. For the purpose of identifying the first hexagram, ignore the small "x" and "o" marking the changing lines and treat any 6 as an 8 and any 9 as a 7.

3. Jot down the *hexagram number* found at the intersection of its *upper trigram* and *lower trigram*.

   Using theChart of Trigrams and Hexagrams, the number of the first hexagram in the example above is 12.

4. This first hexagram of the Oracle's answer to your inquiry represents the "present situation" and often includes elements of the recent past that have led up to the current circumstances.

   • Turn to the chapter of the book that matches the *hexagram number* and read all the paragraphs preceding *"The Line Changes"* interpretations—this part of the reading reflects the overall situation out of which change is arising.

Using the example above, one would turn to Hexagram 12, which is entitled "Seeing Ahead" and read all the "Image," "Interpretation," "Action," "Intent," and "Summary" text.

5. Now returning to the first hexagram, note any of the line changes that occur therein and jot down where they occur—in the 1ST, the 2ND, the 3RD, the 4TH, the 5TH, or the 6TH line. These line changes represent the specific changes within the present situation that are creating the momentum and direction of change that is leading to future circumstances.

   - Turn to the chapter of the book that matches the *hexagram number* of the *first* hexagram and read the interpretation of any *line changes*—this part of the reading reflects the forces that are generating the changes that will result in the coming situation.

Using the example above, one would turn to Hexagram 12, "Seeing Ahead," and read the interpretive text for the 1st and then 5th lines.

   - *If there are no line changes* (no 6s or 9s) in the first hexagram, then there is no second hexagram emerging from it—this signifies that the present situation will not be changing in the near future.

6. Use a similar method with the second hexagram. Again, jot down the *hexagram number* found at the intersection of its *upper trigram* and *lower trigram.*

Using the Chart of Trigrams and Hexagrams, the number of the second hexagram in the example above is 46.

   - This second hexagram of the Oracle's answer to your inquiry represents the "future situation" and often includes elements of the present that are contributing to future circumstances.

   - Turn to the chapter of this book that matches the *hexagram number* and read the "Image," "Interpretation," "Action," "Intent," and "Summary" paragraphs only—this part of the reading reflects the overall situation that is arising out of the present.

Using the example above, one would turn to Hexagram 46, entitled "Honoring Contentment" and read all the text other than "The Line Changes."

- Because the second hexagram is formed by resolving the changing lines of the first hexagram, the second will *never* have any changing lines and so it is unnecessary to read the interpretive texts for its line changes.

Refer to "How to Consult the Oracle" on page 19 for more details on interpreting the Oracle's answer.

Notes

1. Modern spellings of the *I Ching* and its historically accurate name, *Chou I*, are now rendered *Yijing* and *Zhouyi*, respectively. Because their previous spellings have already entered into popular usage, we use the better known renditions here.

2. Among the great civilizations of ancient Mexico and northern Central America, some of the better known are the Toltec, Olmec, Maya, Aztec, Mixtec, and Zapotec peoples. While each of these peoples had their own version of the *Sacred Calendar*, all of those calendars had the same number (260) of days. The word *Tonalpoalli* is itself a Nahuatl term referring to the Aztec version of the *Sacred Calendar*. Several important pre-contact manuscripts still exist which amply document the inner workings of the *Sacred Calendar* (e.g., *The Laud Codex* and *The Borgia Codex*).

3. There is, for example, the similarity between their divinatory systems, both of which are highly structured and generated by a matrix of fixed mathematical possibilities (based on 64 possibilities in the case of the *I Ching* and 260 possibilities in the case of the *Tonalpoalli*). There is also a pronounced division of the world into two creative forces that form complementary halves and account for the continual re-creation of the world (generalized as *yin* and *yang* in the *I Ching* and *feminine* and *masculine* in the *Tonalpoalli*). Both ancient cultures also have strong shamanic traditions that utilize the model of the *warrior* to facilitate the spiritual training of individuals (traditions found throughout most of ancient Asia and the Americas). In addition, both ancient cultures

developed written languages that were pictorial in nature (developing as *ideograms* in ancient China and as standardized *glyphs* in ancient Mexico).

4. Shaughnessy, Edward L, *I Ching: The Classic Of Changes.* pp. 2–5. New York, Ballantine Books, 1996.

5. Wilhelm, Hellmut. *Change: Eight Lectures on the I Ching.* In Hellmut Wilhelm and Wilhelm, Richard, *Understanding the I Ching: The Wilhelm Lectures on the Book of Changes,* pp. 16–17. Princeton: Bollingen, 1995.

6. *Ibid.*

7. Shaughnessy, Edward L, *I Ching: The Classic of Changes.* pp. 14–17. New York, Ballantine Books, 1996.

8. Ibid, p. 18.

REMEMBER: *The **1st line** corresponds with the **first throw** of the coins and the **bottom line** of the hexagram; **the 6th line** corresponds with the **sixth throw** and the **top line** of the hexagram. **Read the line changes for your situation in order from bottom to top.***

EXAMPLE	LINE	FIRST HEXAGRAM	→	SECOND HEXAGRAM	
	6TH	8 — —	→	— —	
	5TH	6 —x—	→	———	UPPER TRIGRAM
	4TH	7 ———	→	———	
	3RD	8 — —	→	— —	
	2ND	7 ———	→	———	LOWER TRIGRAM
	1ST	9 ——o—	→	— —	

64 KEYS TO
INSPIRED ACTION IN
THE NEW WORLD

THE TOLTEC
I CHING

PROVOKING
CHANGE

IMAGE | A male warrior dances with the storm, holding a lightning bolt in one hand and a feather in the other. Where the lightning bolt forks, it takes the form of a serpent of fire, light, and energy. The rattles around his ankles make thunder every time his feet strike the ground and his eyes are fixed on the sky above.

INTERPRETATION | This hexagram represents the great forces essential to creating a new beginning. The male warrior symbolizes the way of testing and training human nature that increases its versatility and fortitude. The lightning bolt symbolizes the focused application of action and intent that provokes dramatic change. That it takes the form of a serpent of fire, light, and energy means that your vision is part of a living creative force whose movement shatters all that is cold, dark, and stagnant. The dance symbolizes a personal ritual that connects you to creation's underlying rhythm of movement and resistance. Dancing with the sky, the storm, the lightning, means that you can sense the rhythmic force of love surrounding you as the feminine and masculine creative forces continue to create and sustain the spark of life within the night of matter. Making thunder in the sky, making earthquakes in the land means that your actions trigger a great explosion of potential which, although it cannot be seen, sets in motion ramifications great enough to change what has come before. Holding the feather means that you are rightly connected to the higher, celestial, forces of the sky, while holding the serpent means that you are rightly connected to the lower, terrestrial, forces of the earth. Taken together, these symbols mean that your actions break up the inertia of the old and set in motion events that cannot yet be envisioned.

ACTION | The masculine half of the spirit warrior guides the movement and energy of the unseen forces, stirring them up and then setting them in motion, calling them forth and then directing them against places where *benefit* is dammed up and unable to follow its natural course. Where greed, ambition, hatred, and contrariness are allowed to fester, true *need* goes unmet and people suffer unnecessarily. The spirit warrior provokes change in order to break up stagnation and release pent-up creative energies, freeing up *benefit* so that it might achieve a new equilibrium and flow to all. Before action, there is a heartfelt *need* whose power is so great that it moves you to act on its behalf. After action, you find that the *benefit* you helped instigate has taken on a life of its own and no longer depends on your efforts for its continuation. Because you are inspired by the ancients' vision of a balanced and harmonious way of life, you win the hearts of others. Because you place the interests of the whole ahead of your own, you help eradicate the selfishness, self-interest, and self-centeredness that has lead to the present impasse. Because you deliberately tip the scales so that they might right themselves again, the stagnation of the old is replaced by a new, dynamic, equilibrium.

INTENT | Whether the stagnation is internal or external, familiarize yourself with its inner workings, its strengths and weaknesses, whom it answers to and who depend on it, what it ignores and what it overreacts to, the passion of its allies and opponents. As a pattern of weak points and blind spots emerges, focus your aim on provoking the greatest possible change using the least possible force. Do not be concerned if you cannot match the strength or resources of others: If you are in the right, then allies will join your cause. Your endeavor succeeds because you purify your intent to sincerely strive solely to see *benefit* moving freely among all.

SUMMARY | Matters must not go on the way they are. It is as if a rock has been placed atop a seedling and must be removed if the plant is to grow. Your search to fulfill your potential will provide the fuel to break up the stultifying effect of stagnation. Study the way things end and you will find the pressure points to force a new beginning. Set aside personal ambition, act for the common good.

THE LINE CHANGES

1ST   The window of opportunity opens—you are poised to ride this wave all the way to the far shore. While others alternate between disbelief and relief, you are learning lessons that will serve you well. When lightning and thunder occur in the same moment, what follows afterward is the ecstatic life.

2ND   Too much change too soon from an unexpected quarter unnerves you when your long-held territory is suddenly claimed by another. Absorb the shock and welcome the newcomer in—such dramatic changes don't last long. Wear critics down with cooperation—don't adopt a siege mentality.

3RD   Your faults are pointed out but you feel compelled to justify them. Instead of correcting them and restoring the peace, you attack those who rightly criticize you. With all the strength of your position, you are still acting out of an internal weakness—this is the road of defeat.

4TH   The initial explosion of thunder is the loudest—it grows fainter with each echo. The momentum of change slows to a crawl as your opponents devise countermoves to your own. Try to maintain the initial pace of change and you'll find yourself hopelessly outnumbered and cornered.

5TH   The critics are more persistent than you imagined and now your obstinacy comes back on you. The merit of your actions is called into question and your reputation is badly damaged. You still have the support of those above and so you will weather this storm—but rough seas lie ahead.

6TH   When the strong lose to the weak it is because of inferior ethics—when the large fail to absorb the small it is because of stubborn prejudice. Make concessions now and sue for peace. This works because all concerned are exhausted by the struggle and long for a reasonable resolution.

SENSING
CREATION

IMAGE | A female warrior is naked, immersed in water and surrounded by flowers. A wellspring of water rises from between her hands. The water drops are drawn as beads of jade in order to portray the precious nature of that which sustains life.

INTERPRETATION | This hexagram represents the great courage essential to creating a meaningful life. The female warrior symbolizes the way of nurturing and encouraging human nature that increases its sensitivity and loving-kindness. Being naked means that nothing stands between you and the world. Being immersed in water means that you plunge wholeheartedly into the spirit of that which nurtures all. Being surrounded by flowers means that you perceive the perfection of the world as it truly is. Each moment blossoms perfect and whole, then passes like a fading flower—each perfection born into the world must die. The wellspring of water symbolizes the inexhaustible source of courage that allows you to use your awareness of mortality to more profoundly experience the joy and sorrow inherent within every encounter. In this sense, the flowers and the water signify not only the wisdom attained through experience, but the aesthetic sensibilities to be moved by a beauty and truth not always apparent to others. Taken together, these symbols mean that you open your spirit to the overwhelming perfection of the world and share your vision with all you touch.

ACTION | The feminine half of the spirit warrior collects the movement and energy of the unseen forces, calming them and bringing them together in harmony, making a place for them to gather strength and then making that source of *benefit* open and available to all. Where past injustices and resentments survive to poison the well of *benefit*, true *need* goes unmet and people suffer unnecessarily: The spirit warrior fosters a climate of forgiveness and reconciliation, reuniting those whose hearts have become estranged and dissolving the tensions and insecurities that have prevented people from coexisting in harmony and mutual understanding. Before action, the passions breeding distrust and discord appear too strong and too deeply entrenched to be overcome. After action, the *benefit* you help cultivate results in a greater union of good will, hope, and creativity. You succeed where others fail because you rely on the warrior's refined sensibilities to guide you rather than on past experiences. You succeed where others fail because you reflect generosity in every thought, word, and deed rather than demanding that others first prove their worth. You succeed where others fail because you cleanse yourself of all ill will rather than harboring any spiritual intent that might poison the well of *benefit* that you are become.

INTENT | Whether the struggle is internal or external, work to increase your sensitivity to the realms of nature, human nature, and spirit. Because people differ only in the degree of their sensitivity to the One Spirit, continue to open your perceptions to more and more sublime thoughts, feelings, memories, and sensations. By recognizing that you are filled with the source of nurturance, you can calmly let all your adaptations arise from it. By giving form to the source of nurturance, you can respond to things with dignity, patience, joy, and appreciation. Because your sensitivity to the world is your strength, you can find the way to restore harmony and progress where others find only opposition and antagonism. Make the well-being of others your goal right now and you can build a coalition of allies to undertake even greater endeavors in the future. Avoid taking sides, work to bring them together. Cultivate trust in the early stages of discord, rely on your lack of self-interest in its later stages. You succeed because you bring future *benefit* to those separated by the past.

SUMMARY | The beauty and loving-kindness you seek are within your reach. Let go of obsolete opinions and dogma handed down to you from others. Find that which allows you to share happiness with others and you will achieve greater freedom and creativity. Focus on the healing of old wounds, promote the forgiving of old wrongs. Set aside personal ambition, act for the common good.

THE LINE CHANGES

1ST   Being a realist, you are optimistic—people have harmed each other and nature for millennia, so you do not react every time humanity fails to live up to its potential. Its successes, though, give you faith in the overall refinement of human nature. Hope, like fear, is contagious—now is the time for hope.

2ND   Being trustworthy, you are trusting—you do not second guess the intentions of your partners or doubt the propriety of their motivations. Although this causes you some harm occasionally, in the long run it makes for wonderful relationships. Expect the best of people and they will reciprocate.

3RD   Being overwhelmed, you are desperate—even if you can't gain the respect of your peers, do not try to appeal to their self-interest. These are ethical people and they would reject such overtures. You are out of place—you were too optimistic about your fit with this project.

4TH   Being intellectual, you are brooding—although you want to believe in the goodness of people, this situation forces you to confront the worst of human nature. Your intent is good but you are not cut out for this. Serving those with less severe wounds will seal your happiness.

5TH   Being sincere, you are susceptible—you may have a superior position but you must rely on the character and advice of others now more than ever. If you are not aware that people may be advocating instead of informing, you will fail. You must be skeptical to sustain your optimism.

6TH   Being tolerant, you are exploited—clever people take advantage of you but do not benefit from their deceit. Do not change your demeanor just because some fail the test—keep casting your net for the rarest creature in the sea. You know people are self-serving but you are looking for the exception.

RECOGNIZING
ANCESTRY

IMAGE | An ancient spirit, part woman and part tree, wears a necklace of jade beads and holds in her heart the shining sun. She is consulting the Oracle by tossing multi-colored kernels of corn onto a woven reed mat and gesturing for us to read the answer there.

INTERPRETATION | The tree is a symbol of the lineage from which all seeds come. The woman is a symbol of the birth and nourishing of human beings. Taken together, this ancient spirit symbolizes the common ancestry of all human beings—an ancestry that extends back to the great creation wherein all beings find their shared origin. For this reason, it is a symbol of your spiritual lineage and your connection to the first creator. The necklace of jade beads is a symbol of humanity itself, whose generations of children are tied together in the circular thread of time and life. The sun in the center, in the heart, symbolizes the source of light and life and love, of understanding and strength and communion. Taken together, the necklace and sun symbolize the responsibility each generation of humanity has in the work of continuing the creation of the world. The oracle is a symbol of divining the future by investigating the unseen forces at work in the present. The reed mat is a symbol of worldly wisdom, which is woven of all the experiences and possibilities of life. Taken together, these symbols mean that you are a descendant of a great spiritual lineage, putting its teachings into practice and carrying its vision forward for the coming generations.

ACTION | The feminine half of the spirit warrior calls your masculine half to open his heart and feel himself part of a spiritual lineage as old as creation. She calls him to awaken to the presence of the unseen forces of spirit and to hold sacred this mysterious creation within which he journeys. She calls on him to reunite in a higher and more creative unity by complementing her nurturing nature with his own purposeful nature. By combining these halves of your dual nature in the right proportions, you can concoct a spiritual medicine at this time that will bring great *benefit* to all around you and, thereby, to yourself. This is a time for recognizing that you walk the same road as your spiritual ancestors, that you are undertaking a journey they undertook, that your footprints often match their own. Now is a time when the voice of the great-great-great-grandmother is especially strong, so you can approach her as you would the world spirit itself and receive the wisdom and companionship of all the spirit warriors who share this pilgrimage with you. By filling your heart now with the presence and the guidance of the ancestors, you can pursue your lifework with complete and utter faith in the course you have taken. Do not doubt that there exists a lineage of immortal spirits nor that you are a seed of that tree.

INTENT | When strength is not tempered with loving-kindness, people become headstrong and arrogant, holding to obsolete habits of thought and feeling long after they have outlived their purpose. Become familiar with this pattern of imbalance and learn to recognize the signs of its worsening—frustration, indignation, and isolation—so that you can intervene at the right moment to break the fever, so to speak, by reintroducing the masculine half to its complementary feminine half. Whether you find this imbalance in yourself or others, you can provide a counterbalance to the *need* arising from a growing sense of aloneness by calling attention to the inner path, the route by which spirit warriors travel between this world and the universal homeland in the inner world of spirit. Following this path toward the innermost horizon, you re-enter the community of the one great spiritual lineage uniting every warrior in every time.

SUMMARY | What you reject at one time is what you eventually respect. The roots of the human spirit run deep and wide—take great care to respect every lineage, be genuinely open to the teachings of every tradition. Let your sense of spirituality grow and evolve over time. Like strings vibrating to the same note, recognize your spiritual ancestry as that which resonates with your deepest memories. Work diligently to put your new understandings into practice: Express the essence in all your thoughts and deeds.

The Line Changes

1ST Your search for ways to improve yourself is praiseworthy—but don't become so enamored with the search that you forget the goal. Neither new ideas nor attention from instructors is it. Put what you have already learned into practice consistently before learning anything new.

2ND Your effort to fulfill all your roles and responsibilities is praiseworthy—but it must not take away from the time you spend with those closest to you. Seize this opportunity to strengthen the bonds between you. This journey is intended to be shared with boon companions.

3RD Your effort to get along with your peers is praiseworthy—but too much familiarity creates difficulties. There are always those you cannot get along with, which results in personality conflicts if proper boundaries don't exist. Keep your role and personality separate.

4TH Your effort to attack the same subject on many fronts is praiseworthy—but too many projects dilute your energy. Focus on the one nearest completion. Finish it successfully and then build on that success with each of the others in turn.

5TH Your effort to provide for your circle is praiseworthy—but it must not be achieved at the expense of others around you. Instead of negotiating for ever-increasing advantages, solidify your relations with the other side by helping it prosper, too. Benefiting others will benefit you.

6TH Your search for self-realization is praiseworthy—but it must not become an intellectual pursuit of concepts and doctrines. Try to stop the inner speech for extended periods of time. Translate noble thoughts into felt emotions.

MIRRORING
WISDOM

IMAGE | A male warrior faces an eagle and a jaguar, who are teaching him the lessons of nature so that he can successfully respond to every circumstance he encounters. The speech glyphs are multi-colored to depict the different dimensions of nature's lessons.

INTERPRETATION | The eagle is a symbol of the day, of the masculine force, and represents the direct approach to circumstances. The jaguar is a symbol of the night, of the feminine force, and represents the indirect approach to circumstances. Taken together, they symbolize a balanced and harmonious way of life, meaning that you are able to use both direct action to confront circumstances and indirect action to mature circumstances, tailoring your responses to the *need* of the time. The male warrior is a symbol of the way of testing and training human nature that increases its versatility and fortitude. The speech of the eagle and jaguar symbolize the lessons that can be learned from the primary forces of nature by those who listen respectfully. Taken together, these symbols mean that you succeed in your fierce determination to train your emotions, thoughts, and will to act in concert to overcome every hardship.

ACTION | The masculine half of the spirit warrior calls your feminine half to open her heart and feel herself part of a spiritual initiation as old as creation. He calls her to awaken to her innate capacity to change things and to view this lifetime as a bridge across which she journeys. He calls on her to reunite in a higher and more creative unity by complementing his purposeful nature with her own nurturing nature. By combining these halves of your dual nature in the right proportions, you can acquire the wisdom of the old ones, who learned from nature both how to adapt to change, as well as how to anticipate it. This is a time for studying the behavior of nature and its relationships in order to better understand the behavior and relationships of human nature and spirit. Now is a time when the voice of the great-great-great-grandfather is especially strong, so you can approach him as you would the sky spirit itself and receive the eternal meanings behind all of nature's symbols. By filling your heart now with the intent to travel the ancient path of wisdom, you can pursue your lifework knowing that you are helping build the road of perfect freedom. Do not doubt that spirit dwells within nature nor that it speaks in a language understood by your heart nor that it leaves tracks in its passing that you may follow.

INTENT | When loving-kindness is not tempered with strength, people become dependent and resentful, trusting others too much and then growing disillusioned when their own good will is not reciprocated. Become familiar with this pattern of imbalance and learn to recognize its signs of worsening—apathy, helplessness, and desperation—so that you can intervene at the right moment to break the fever, so to speak, by reintroducing the feminine half to its complementary masculine half. Whether you find this imbalance in yourself or others, you can provide a counterbalance to the *need* arising from a growing sense of being unfulfilled by calling attention to the outer path, the route by which spirit warriors train to prove their immortality by overcoming every mortal obstacle. Following this path toward the outermost horizon, you pass through every ordeal like an ancient tree passing through another season.

SUMMARY | No matter how well you see when things are as clear as day, the eagle sees better. No matter how well you see when things are as obscure as night, the jaguar sees better. Keep your heart filled with humility so you can keep learning from your spirit guides. Wisdom cannot blossom among the weeds of opinion, arrogance, laziness, and self-satisfaction. Eliminate nervousness, cultivate calm. Work diligently to achieve goals that appear just beyond your reach: The spirit within nature is the same spirit within you.

THE LINE CHANGES

1ST The first thing to do in establishing new priorities is to abandon the old ones. This means watching your thoughts, words, and actions to determine how influenced they are by the old priorities. Being aware of this influence is like turning on the light to catch robbers in your house red-handed.

2ND Sometimes a crisis is needed to inspire a change of priorities. Someone you count on cannot be counted on, turning your world upside-down. This forces you to find other kinds of relationships that help you adopt new and more constructive priorities—this is the path of the ecstatic life.

3RD The priorities can be changed but old habits of emotion cling like barnacles to the hull of a boat. Just because they are under the surface does not mean they are not real. Look where you feel righteous indignation and resentment—scrape these habits off and you will encounter no resistance.

4TH You must beware of creating a crisis just when everything is going right. By counting on the wrong person at this time you will betray the confidence of all the others who have placed their trust in you. A slip here will result in a long fall—make others prove they share your new priorities.

5TH You carry the weight of your responsibilities well but must still rely on the support and tolerance of close allies to see you through. Your greatness is apparent to all but yourself. Such humility is charming but sometimes appears undignified—your new priorities show you what you serve.

6TH When your new priorities are fully implemented, everything in the world is nourishing. Everything teaches you about the invisible half of nature—and its invisible connections of cause-and-effect that underlie change. You become a source of great comfort, advice, and nourishment to all you touch.

RESTORING
WHOLENESS

IMAGE | An old woman heals a young male warrior, who wears an arrowhead necklace. While she chants an ancient curing song, she places a lizard on his shoulder and administers purifying herbs and water.

INTERPRETATION | This hexagram depicts great *benefit* fulfilling great *need*. The old woman personifies the great-great-great-grandmother, the feminine force of profound wisdom and nurturing, the inner healing force within all, the aged and loving medicine woman. The male warrior personifies the strength and vitality of youth, the great potential of the young, the idealism and insensitivity of the inexperienced, the impatient and reactive nature of the untrained passions. Taken together, they symbolize the exchange of forces needed to heal your old wounds and enable you to bring *benefit* to all around you. The herbs symbolize the feminine medicines of compassion and the understanding of relationships. The arrowhead represents the masculine medicines of single-mindedness and the pursuit of new experiences. Taken together, they depict the exchange of energies whereby the new must be refined by the old and the old must periodically be revitalized by the new. For this reason, the hexagram shows that the young warrior is both a patient and an apprentice of the medicine woman, learning firsthand the ways of restoring natural and original wholeness and thereby bringing much needed energy to the feminine half that has been giving to others for so long. The lizard, the "one who grows back its tail," represents the spiritual medicine of regeneration whereby the original state of wholeness is restored. The medicinal herbs and water together represent the purifying and cleansing away of the useless, the wasteful, and that which only confuses and drags down the original energy of body, mind, and spirit. Taken together, these symbols mean that you reclaim your spiritual birthright of indivisible wholeness.

ACTION | The masculine and feminine halves of the spirit warrior replenish one another. It is a time for seeking new experiences that will broaden your vistas and deepen your joy of life. Your innate wisdom and compassion do not have their source in thought but, rather, in life—they are not replenished by good intentions but, rather, by meaningful experiences. In order for a well to bring *benefit* to others, it must tap into the unseen river of *benefit* flowing beneath the surface of the world of the senses. Take no comfort in your accomplishments or knowledge now. Instead, look to your *need* and pursue new interests that hold the possibility of discovering more meaningful joy in this lifetime. Take a more playful and spontaneous approach to matters for a while, confident that what you find will reinvigorate your more serious efforts to nurture others. It is not necessary to know ahead of time what new interest will prove meaningful—just as following a butterfly might accidentally lead you to a treasure, simply follow whatever captures your attention at present, confident that the creative forces will lead you to the proper goal. Unsettling the beneficial feminine force in this way breaks up routines of thought, feeling, and memory, forcing you to reach a more effective balance between giving and having enough to give. Because you make yourself whole again, you succeed in bringing *benefit* to others likewise seeking to restore their own wholeness.

INTENT | When people's reactions are out of proportion to events, that is a clear signal that an old wound has not fully healed and is being reactivated by present circumstances. Such reactions barely disguise the fact that something in the present is provoking an individual or group to re-live the emotions of an old injury. But disguise it they do, for the impact of many injuries is either long-forgotten or unrecognized. Whether you find this imbalance in yourself or others, the nurturing-medicine of the wise feminine force must be augmented by the directing-medicine of the single-minded masculine force. While it is essential that the wounded warrior be healed through reassurance and loving-kindness, it is just as necessary that the wounded warrior take up the discipline of recognizing that the new is not the old. At the first sign of distress, the wounded warrior must immediately name the present and not allow the past wound to be re-opened. Using the beneficial masculine force in this way allows you to keep the past from infecting the present.

SUMMARY | A forgotten part of you returns and takes the lead in establishing a new sense of inner unity and purpose. Welcome the idealism and vitality of the young masculine warrior back into yourself and then act on your newfound vision of your future. Overconfidence is preferable to timidity at this time. Balance your roles and responsibilities with the new, the exciting, the daring.

THE LINE CHANGES

1ST   The window of opportunity opens—you benefit substantially from the good will of your superiors. Their support means you are able to initiate your project—do not betray their faith in you by giving less of yourself than you promised. Find a way to keep this excitement and gratitude always alive.

2ND   This relationship proves exceptionally beneficial for both of you—you are able to advance because others invite you to approach. Beware of stagnant routines masquerading as real continuity. The art of renewal arises from starting over in surprising ways.

3RD   When times are difficult for nearly everyone, survival justifies benefiting from those with more than enough. But it is imperative that you conduct yourself with integrity and violate no ethics. It is best to have something of real benefit to exchange—but it is essential that you cause no one harm.

4TH   When you have eradicated all personal interest in the outcome of events, so that you never gain any advantage from your opinions, then your advice will be sought by those above and below. Such ethical counsel is hard to find—cultivate it. Such an impartial heart benefits all—nurture it.

5TH   Those who control the allocation of resources must be of the highest character, incapable by nature of playing favorites or rewarding unethical conduct. The judicious allotment of resources revitalizes growth and stimulates prosperity. Target those endeavors that produce more than they consume.

6TH   When renewal is exploited to provide an excuse for making self-serving changes, then others take an antagonistic position. No matter how it may be justified, if you take advantage of others, you undercut the very support you will need. Pretend to be more caring and generous until you are.

FOSTERING
SELF-SACRIFICE

IMAGE | A tree is struck by lightning and breaks apart. The upper part of the tree falls away and is carried off by the storm, accompanied by an eagle ascending into the sky with it. A serpent descends into the earth, carrying the trunk of the tree away with it. Only those most delicate roots of the tree that extend out and become the veins of the ancestors' hand ultimately remain.

INTERPRETATION | This hexagram represents a time of great change that holds no immediate opportunities for you to advance. The tree represents the continuity of a way of life. The lightning storm represents circumstances beyond people's control. Taken together, they symbolize the ending of something and a breakdown of customary routines, polarizing people and making them insecure and distrustful. The upper part of the tree flying off into the sky with the eagle spirit means that those above have noble intentions and pursue them without compromise. The lower part of the tree descending into the earth with the serpent spirit means that those below have noble intentions and pursue them without compromise. The roots transforming into the veins of the ancestors' hand mean that true continuity can only be found at this time in your grasp, your personal comprehension, of the inner path of the ancients. Taken together, these symbols mean that you wait for the turbulence of the times to calm, neither revealing your intentions nor acting on your decisions.

ACTION | It is a time for experiencing the ancestors' way of life as a living vision of spiritual work. Even though many around you view spirit as a relic of primitive belief, you must resist the movement toward materialism and cynicism. There are dramatic fluctuations in gain and loss now and people are unable to guess where fortune and misfortune will strike next. While people may make a show of unity and cooperation, behind the scenes individuals and factions compete fiercely for advantage. Because all sides perceive their motives justified, they resist reconciliation with all their might. In such a climate, it is easy to be swept up in the passions of the moment and dragged back and forth indefinitely. Because you see your way of life as a vital act of spiritual work, however, you are moved neither by ambition nor antagonism. Seeking to bring the greatest *benefit* to the greatest number, you do not hesitate to place the *need* of others above your own. Restraining the impulsive and determined nature of the masculine force in this way strengthens and ennobles your spirit, forming the seeds of future success for your endeavor.

INTENT | One of the ancients' great teachings is that acting out of self-interest to the detriment of the whole injures all. Because profit brings gain for one at the expense of many and *benefit* brings gain for many at the expense of one, the logic of *benefit* is superior to the logic of profit. Because self-interest cannot injure the whole without injuring oneself and self-sacrifice cannot benefit the whole without benefiting oneself, the logic of self-sacrifice is superior to the logic of self-interest. Do not be tempted to make a move at this time, as your motives will be called into question and you will become embroiled in conflict and hostility. Wait patiently, hone your skills, broaden your experience: By not acting prematurely, you will be respected and sought after when the window of opportunity next opens. While every ending begets a new beginning, the moment of that begetting cannot be rushed.

SUMMARY | In the midst of chaos and confusion, hold firm to your belief in serving others. Focus on the well-being of those around you and your needs will be met. Set an example by refusing to worry about things outside your control. Do not try to advance at this time. Be an asset to others. Strengthen your foundation, broaden your alliances. The momentum is against you for a while longer.

THE LINE CHANGES

1ST   An all-or-nothing attitude is admirable at the end but regrettable at the beginning. Expecting immediate trust and plain speech without shared experiences is naive and opens you to manipulation. Do not underestimate others or overestimate yourself.

2ND   The situation is much more complicated than you first thought, the tangle of relationships more knotted than you imagined. Whatever you say to one will be repeated to all—show too much weakness or too much strength to one and it will be reported to all. This will be a long, slow march.

3RD   You cannot overstep the bounds without looking amateurish. You cannot think of this as a stepping stone to something better without ruining your reputation. You are boxed in and will lose face no matter what you do—when you cannot move or stand still, it is time to learn to do something new.

4TH   You have taken on a hopeless task—the agreement you seek is not to be fashioned among all these competing interests. Each faction has taken a position long ago that they cannot relinquish. You arrived too late—best to leave early.

5TH   Holding a position of strength, still you respond to all with graciousness and respect. When winning allies, you brood like a mother hen—when confronting opponents, you move like a rushing tiger. Now, what will you forge?

6TH   When there is a shakeup beyond your control, the agitation and uncertainty filling the air make it impossible to accomplish anything. If you are closely aligned with the past, it is best to leave now. If you are new on the scene, you may find a place when the dust settles.

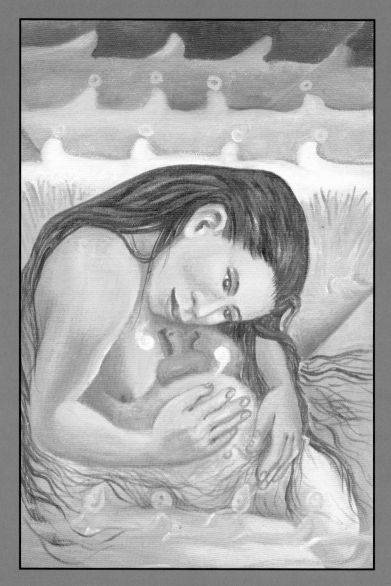

COMPELLING
MOTIVE

IMAGE | A female warrior who is close to giving birth bathes tranquilly in a lake. From her womb there emerges a heart, with whom she is having a dialog. The speech glyphs are colored white to signify their purity and dignity, the water drops are drawn as jade beads in order to portray the precious nature of that which sustains life.

INTERPRETATION | The female warrior symbolizes the way of nurturing and encouraging human nature that increases its sensitivity and loving-kindness. That she gives birth means that you bring something new into the world. The lake symbolizes the tranquility and serenity found in communing with nature and spirit. Bathing symbolizes purifying the thoughts, feelings, and intentions. Taken together, these symbols mean you are beginning a new endeavor that you truly believe will bring *benefit* to others. A heart emerging from the womb means that you love what you are creating—and feel loved by it. Having a dialog with the newborn heart means that you actively speak to it of your hopes and intentions—and actively listen to its vision of its purpose and potential. Taken together, these symbols mean that the spirit of your lifework sustains and cares for you and your unborn creation—and that your vision and purpose are part of a larger effort dedicated to protecting that which is most valuable.

ACTION | The feminine half of the spirit warrior does not tarry at the crossroads. When the spirit of the heart calls, you must answer. Even if the calling comes when you are least prepared for it, it is your calling and cannot be ignored. Those who come across an acorn but see instead an oak tree have glimpsed the next part they have to play in the unfolding of creation. If you set aside other goals and wholeheartedly pursue this new direction, then you will find greater meaning, happiness, and success in life. It is essential to speak to the spirit of your endeavor, to treat it with respect and love and caring, to nurture it until it is whole and strong enough to emerge from the womb of *benefit*. You find that which deserves to be preserved when you find an inner *need* that you share with others. It is likewise essential to listen to the spirit of your endeavor, to allow yourself to be respected and loved and cared for, to be nurtured until you are whole and strong enough to emerge from the womb of *benefit*. Just as an infant still in the womb may communicate with its mother, sharing its perceptions and protecting her with its intuitions, the spirit of your endeavor guides you to a future that is safe and filled with opportunity for growth and fulfillment.

INTENT | Before acting externally, it is necessary to act internally— before making your decision known to others, it is necessary to incubate your plans in private. For this reason, it can be a frustrating time, one in which preparation can be mistaken for procrastination and gestation for inaction. This kind of impatience must be subdued by immersing yourself in the feminine spirit of water, which nourishes without bias. It can, however, also be time of timidity, one in which real procrastination can be mistaken for preparation and true inaction for gestation. Such hesitancy must be subdued by immersing yourself in the masculine spirit of water, which rushes headlong towards the sea without interruption. Once you have made the emotional decision to change direction, you must not reveal your intention until you are ready to act—but once you have revealed your intention, you must not allow anything to deter you from acting.

SUMMARY | What you are trying to do is important, not just for your own future but that of others, as well. If you remain true to your loving and nurturing nature, you will enjoy real success. If you succumb to mistrustful and self-serving feelings, however, your hopes will not be fulfilled. Do not hesitate to pursue a new opportunity at this time, no matter how suddenly or unexpectedly it arises.

THE LINE CHANGES

1ST   Cautious to the point of being timid, accommodating to the point of being conciliatory—this serves well enough for now but you will need to be more decisive and purposeful in the time ahead. The kind of confidence that is needed cannot be faked, however. Build on your real strengths.

2ND   A truly great partnership—it balances the strengths of both. Harmony is not always consonant—it is often filled with necessary dissonance that resolves into a higher consonance. As if fated from the beginning, this partnership will benefit you both and, more importantly, many, many others.

3RD   Assertive to the point of being aggressive, opinionated to the point of being inflexible—though you do not show this side of yourself to others, it is the underlying attitude responsible for your failures. You cannot fake a change of heart. Allow your burdens to make you more open.

4TH   Overall, you are contributing positively to a positive situation—you have endurance and admirable talents. There is, however, the perennial danger of becoming dependent on those you serve—don't let the fact that you know this keep you from being wary. Roles must be preserved at all costs.

5TH   A short-term gain can often have long-term costs that negate what value there might have been at first. It is easy to get infatuated with an idea, goal, or person—but it is harder to get out of trouble than it was getting into it. Such advice falls on deaf ears, though, and no real harm results.

6TH   Others encourage you to take up a cause, appealing to your sense of justice and compassion. From where you stand you cannot see where this river takes you but your first inclination is to leap in. This may be a worthwhile cause but you must be prepared to sacrifice personally if you take it up.

HARMONIZING
DUALITY

IMAGE | Two faces, one of a male warrior and the other of a female warrior, complement one another in perfect balance and harmony. The masculine face is that of the wind, whose color is hot and active. The feminine face is that of water, whose color is cool and reflective. The moving ends of the wind are drawn mimicking speech glyphs of fire in order to portray its power to instigate change. The waves of the water are drawn ending in jade beads in order to portray the precious nature of that which nourishes life and spirit.

INTERPRETATION | This hexagram represents the duality of forces within everyone and everything. The female warrior symbolizes the bringing forth of the diamond of creation, whereas the male warrior symbolizes its cutting and polishing. The union of the two faces means that you bring the two halves of the warrior's spirit into ever greater balance and harmony. The confluence of wind and water means that you bring your intent into ever greater accord with the visible and invisible currents of creation. The conjunction of the hot dry wind and the cold damp water means that you bring a spiritual remedy to an ever greater range of those imbalances of forces which cause all ills. Taken together, these symbols mean that you harness the contradictory and complementary forces within yourself in order to achieve ever greater creativity, contentment, wisdom, and compassion.

ACTION | The masculine and feminine halves of the spirit warrior unite in mutual reverence. In order to be true to ourselves, to genuinely know ourselves and fulfill our true potential, it is necessary to acknowledge that each of us contains our own contradiction. Failure to acknowledge our true nature slows our progress, sometimes to the point of wasting an entire lifetime. Because creation evolves by fusing related halves into a new whole, this is a time for consciously experiencing the never-changing nature of the true self. Because creation evolves by splitting each whole into new halves, this is a time for consciously experiencing the ever-changing nature of the true self. Those who do not experience firsthand the unity within duality come to favor one half of their nature over the other, too timid and insecure to achieve real independence. Those who do not experience firsthand the duality within unity grow self-satisfied and complacent, too vain and arrogant to believe there are limits they have yet to transcend. As your masculine half and feminine half achieve equilibrium, you respond to events according to their *need* rather than your own strengths, skills, or preconceptions. Just as the lake harmonizes with the wind's movement by making waves, all that you encounter will harmonize with your inner equilibrium by bringing their own internal forces into better balance.

INTENT | Before harmonizing the core, it is necessary to harmonize the surface—before cultivating inner independence, it is necessary to decrease dependence on external stimuli. This is not the time to seek fulfillment from the outside. Rather, deepen your appreciation of the commonplace, taking care to bore the senses and disinterest the intellect. As you withdraw your focus from the world of dualities around you, shift your attention to the world of dualities within you. Identify by feel both the bright ascending clear energy and the dark descending turbid energy, following the way in which they shift between one another as they take turns expressing themselves through your feelings, thoughts, and actions. As you gain greater familiarity with their alternating movement, apply your intent to one or the other, adding to its momentum just as you would add increments of weight to one side or the other of a balance in order to make the two sides equal. Continuing to apply this method allows you to bring your inner duality to a stable and harmonious balance—a point from which you are able to shift from one half of the warrior's spirit to the other with a minimum of effort. Through such self-discipline you harness the forces of the spirit warrior's complementary halves, expressing yourself through their marriage rather than being expressed by their pendulum-like swings from one extreme to the other. The *benefit* you engender in this way is like air and water to the unseen forces.

SUMMARY | Do not take things personally—keep in mind that the pendulum of action-and-backlash swings according to universal laws. Work diligently to neither give offense nor take offense. Focus on how you are treating others rather than how they are treating you at this time. Subtly influence the actions of those you cannot change outright by allying yourself with their better nature.

THE LINE CHANGES

1ST   The purity of intent of a newborn—you are incapable of intentionally harming anyone or anything. The well-being of all forms of life is your passionate concern—you harbor no mean-spiritedness, cynicism, or pessimism anywhere within you. Do not ever let go your trustworthiness.

2ND   The purity of intent of a parent—you cannot but fulfill your responsibilities to those who depend on you. Nonetheless, you are loved for who you are and not for what you do—you are most fortunate to be accepted by those close to you. Keep the mutual concern circulating among you.

3RD   The purity of intent of a sibling—others may feel compelled to compete but you must not follow suit. Reassure them over time by simply holding your position and letting them advance or expand to their hearts' content. They will come to trust you and be valuable allies in the future.

4TH   The purity of intent of a teacher—your every word and action is a lesson to those around you. How do you encourage others to strike the road of individuality and still listen to you? How do you show others that your devotion to them is part and parcel of your devotion to the higher?

5TH   The purity of intent of a guardian—you can ask those below to sacrifice for the good of the whole and they gladly comply. This brings everyone together in a unity of purpose. Make no ethical missteps and the strong support you enjoy from below will not evaporate.

6TH   The purity of intent of a grandparent—your most trustworthy advisers do not just tell you what you want to hear. Listen to those with real life experience and change your demeanor accordingly. Rid yourself of every shred of hypocrisy and your every word will ring true.

UPROOTING
FEAR

IMAGE | A male warrior, wearing war paint and a jaguar headdress, stands at the mouth of a cave and utters a battle cry that sounds like a jaguar's roar. In one hand he holds the power of the lightning and its thunder and fire. His other arm is clenched, forming a shield of obsidian knives. The flight of arrows is broken and stopped in flight.

INTERPRETATION | This hexagram represents the indomitable intent of those who will not be overcome by fear or insecurity. The male warrior symbolizes the way of testing and training human nature that increases its versatility and fortitude. His war paint and battle cry mean that you do not hesitate to show your resolve through direct speech and direct action. The cavern and jaguar headdress, both symbols of the feminine half of the spirit warrior, mean that you do not hesitate to conceal your deeper intentions within the feints and stratagems of indirect action. Taken together, these symbols mean that you withstand every inner and outer test of nerves the way a mountain withstands every individual raindrop. Wielding the lightning's fire and thunder means that you can concentrate the energy of the creative forces and direct it toward making matters known, using the power of fire to illuminate and the power of thunder to resound. Forming a shield of obsidian knives means that you invoke the law of equal action and reaction, defending yourself solely by adopting the patient strength of those who no longer try to keep destructive people from destroying themselves. Stopping the arrows in flight means that the spiritual protection you cultivate succeeds in making you impervious to harm. Taken together, these symbols mean that you have prepared well for this battle and have nothing to fear.

ACTION | The masculine half of the spirit warrior protects the feminine half from physical, emotional, and spiritual harm. Only a wholehearted commitment to the proper course of action will stand you in good stead—only through clarity of vision, firmness of will, and consistency of action will you be able to act with the courage and conviction needed to prevail against those in the wrong. When we can no longer make excuses for oppression and coercion, then we find what it is that is worth fighting for. It is at just such a juncture that we commit to a course of action that improves our lives, refines our character, and broadens our compassion. This is a time for hardening your heart against even the slightest of fears and closing your mind to even the remotest possibilities of failure. Take up the symbols of this hexagram and make yourself like this spirit warrior and you will not only pass through the trial unscathed, but you will bring *benefit* to others in ways impossible to imagine at present. Because your motive is pure and your reasoning sound, you act without doubt or hesitation.

INTENT | By pulling out the weeds of fear and indecision when they first appear, you will acquire the inner power to break up stagnation and free up *benefit* so that it might fulfill its corresponding *need* once again. In such a time, it is necessary to coordinate your forces in response to events. When you must confront matters, do so unemotionally, speaking the truth without exaggeration or distortion. When you are attacked, defend your spirit in private without responding to taunts or intimidation in public. Act with the daring of one who has gambled everything on a single throw of the dice, advancing when you are expected to withdraw and withdrawing when you are expected to advance. Do not hesitate to make allies of those within the opponent's camp, thereby allowing doubt and fear to take root among those who sought to sow it.

SUMMARY | Your path takes you into unknown lands without any clear sense of where you are being led. You are fully committed to this course now and there is no turning back. Set your will firmly on the goal and banish all worrying and second thoughts from your mind. All this is meant to be, so proceed with unshakeable confidence and optimism. Move like a jaguar among rabbits.

THE LINE CHANGES

1ST Those in power are arrogant and care nothing for the well-being of those under them. This makes it a tempting time to mobilize popular support in an effort to oust such villains. But such efforts can succeed only if supported nearly unanimously—proceed slowly and seek more allies.

2ND Conflicting interests tug at you, forcing you to decide between them. You cannot belong to both groups, so you will have to choose between personal ambition and more altruistic motives. Don't drag your feet—the tension will last only as long as you remain undecided.

3RD Those in power are distant and do not care that people strain without end at meaningless work. No one seems to be able to take the reins and guide matters back on course—true leaders would admit their mistakes and ask for popular support in correcting them. Maintain your neutrality for now.

4TH Your motives are noble and your ambitions worthwhile, so you need to investigate fully before committing to this proposal. Do not mar your reputation by associating with those of questionable ethics. The best ending arises from the best beginning—give preference to proven performance.

5TH Those in power have isolated themselves and grown deaf to any voice but their own. Do not call down retaliation upon yourself by speaking out at this time. Rather than trying to start any new projects, now is the time to withdraw and wait for the old to collapse under its own weight.

6TH It is possible to become dependent on anything, so that even a strength becomes a weakness if relied on too much. Examine your habits of body, emotion, memory, and thought, resolving to rid yourself of destructive ones. The time-tested method is to replace them with spiritual leanings.

UNIFYING
INSPIRATION

IMAGE | A female warrior gazes at the moon and paints what she experiences. In the sky, ancient creative forces sing of perfection and the moon echoes their song. Lightning falls from the sky, providing the warrior with the creative energy to paint her vision. The warrior's heart opens and echoes the song of perfection, too. On her paper made of precious tree bark, she paints of the song she hears and of the butterfly of transformation she feels.

INTERPRETATION | This hexagram represents a vision of the wondrous aspirations that can arise from shared experiences. The female warrior symbolizes the way of nurturing and encouraging human nature that increases its sensitivity and loving-kindness. That she paints the moon the way she sees it means that you contemplate the ways in which nature transforms itself and that you give them expression in your life. The moon echoing the song of the creative spirits means that you learn the ways of the unseen forces and make them your own. Painting with lightning means that you give voice to the perfecting power which runs like a thread of continuity from the past, through the present, and to the future. Opening her heart to the song of the unseen forces means that you see into the essence of the world and rejoice in the perfection you perceive underlying the surface of appearances. The warrior's painting is heartfelt but modest, meaning that even our best efforts are incapable of fully capturing the power, scope, and grandeur of our vision. Taken together, these symbols mean that even in an experience as universal as gazing at the moon, you see into its essence and translate its meaning in ways that draw others together in a vision of the true significance and potential of the whole to which they belong.

ACTION | The feminine half of the spirit warrior reawakens the masculine half to the beauty, joy, and truth to be found in sharing *benefit*. Fulfillment is not an intellectual state devoid of emotional conscience or social communion—it is, rather, a state of multiplying *benefit* that strives to overflow its vessel in order to enrich other vessels. So powerful is its sense of purpose that *benefit* will eventually withdraw from those who do not use it to fulfill others. The *need* here is for a sense of purpose itself, for those who are themselves misguided try to guide others and all concerned suffer from the leadership's lack of perspective, compassion, and foresight. The heart must be filled with a vision of the great endeavor, whose collective purpose explains past events and actions, increases tolerance and understanding among contemporaries, and prepares meaningful responses to future events. People can sacrifice personal fulfillment indefinitely only if they feel themselves contributing to the fulfillment of something greater than themselves. For this reason, meaningless work in exchange for personal material security cannot hold people enthralled very long—nor can threats of losing such meaningless security force compliance in the long run. This is the time for a positive vision of unity that inspires people to set aside past conflicts, accept and respect one another's potential, and work together toward a goal that ennobles the lives of all concerned. Only when people feel that all partake equally from the pool of resources do they willingly take up as much of the great burden as they can carry. Open your heart to the divine purpose of human life and your vision will be like a torch for others seeking to perfect their part of creation.

INTENT | All those who have ever lived have gazed upon the moon, their dreams and memories and knowledge reflected forever in that mirror of the unseen forces. All those who have ever lived have bathed in the light of the moon, purified by the ancestors' expression of a life in harmony with the world of nature and spirit. Every time the spirit warrior returns to the world, the moon awaits to inspire both the feminine half with an inner calendar for renewing the cycles of creation and the masculine half with an inner light for exploring the infinite night of the unknown. Drawing this hexagram, be grateful you can hear the song of the creative forces, that you can hear the language of creation: Let what you hear echo in your own heart, dialog with it, and let it echo back out in your own thoughts, feelings, words, and actions.

SUMMARY | Do not lose faith in your original vision of truth and beauty and love. Hold to the eternal ideals of the human spirit, continuing to give expression to them in all facets of your life. Your sincerity and persistence in defiance of the odds bring you into contact with a growing number of like-minded warriors. Work hard to keep your alliance open to all who share your vision of unification.

THE LINE CHANGES

1ST   When people are starting over, it is difficult not to feel desperate and needy. However, you have enough at your disposal to make it through this transition time. Become more self-sufficient, overcoming your insecurity and anger, before entering into any new partnerships.

2ND   Do not make your quest for security so important that it overshadows all other facets of your life. Those around you long to bask in the warmth of your light-hearted nature. You cannot prepare for every eventuality but you can make every moment count—fall back on your inner resources.

3RD   When people exaggerate their capabilities and aptitudes, they find themselves in positions beyond their capacity. What appears at first to be a dream-come-true turns into a nightmare. Represent yourself ethically and all will be well—do not, and you harm your reputation for future endeavors.

4TH   When people join together to fulfill a shared vision, their excitement and enthusiasm are palpable. Use the authorization from above to keep everyone motivated and focused on the long-range goal. Only if your resourcefulness results in a finished project will your efforts be judged a success.

5TH   Do not let your impulses get the better of you—this is a time for being practical and prudent, not a time to overextend yourself. You have outgrown this old habit of seeking something new to calm an underlying uneasiness. Set aside comforts and make frugality part of your spiritual practice.

6TH   When people are short-sighted and pursue unearned gain, they deplete their resources and call down hardship upon themselves. When a lack of resourcefulness goes to an extreme, adjustments must follow that balance the scales. Even if the flood is not your fault, you get swept up in it.

ATTRACTING
ALLIES

IMAGE | A corn stalk stands against the sky. In place of ears of corn there grow conch shells, whose song can be heard far and wide. Feminine and masculine spirits use earthen jars to pour water onto the plant from above.

INTERPRETATION | This hexagram depicts sustained and conscientious effort being rewarded with success. Corn symbolizes the food that sustains life. The corn stalk is a symbol of the plowing, sowing, and cultivating that it takes to produce that sustenance. The conch symbolizes hidden power because it is a secretive animal that creates a home of perfect strength and beauty and symmetry, whereas the conch shell, which carries within itself the song of the sea and has since time immemorial been used as a ceremonial trumpet, is a symbol of that which calls people and spirits to gather. Taken together, these symbols mean that your endeavor is laborious but, because it holds the promise of bringing *benefit* to others, does attract the attention of unseen benefactors. The feminine and masculine spirits coming from above symbolize the helping spirits who answer your call. Whereas the earthen jar symbolizes the land's fertility, water coming from above symbolizes rain and the sky's fertility. Taken together, these symbols mean that your masculine half and feminine half are harmoniously balanced, uniting the spirit of purposeful action and the spirit of loving nourishment in a concerted effort to produce *benefit* in harmony with the creative spirits themselves.

ACTION | The masculine and feminine halves of the spirit warrior work together to achieve a goal that ennobles and enriches all. Now is the time to set aside all hope and fear, bearing down on the work itself. If you persist, patiently plowing row after row after row, never looking to the end of the field, setting aside all thoughts of progress, then you will truly master the situation and receive assistance from an unforeseen quarter. By working for the sake of the work rather than your own *need*, you create a history of sincerity and selflessness as significant as any history of your accomplishments, since those who have the power to help you are as interested in your character as they are in your abilities. Yet even thinking about the thoughts of those who might help you is a distraction that can lead you off your path and into the mire of ambition and self-interest. Simply view your endeavor as the daily discharge of a sacred trust, your part in a work that has no foreseeable end. Work hard, perfect your craft, develop your potential, and the reason for taking this path will make itself known. Trust that the unseen forces have taken note of the purity of your intent and, even now, are judging how they might assist in the realization of your vision.

INTENT | When we realize we need help in accomplishing a difficult task, our first impulse is to turn to those who we believe share in our responsibilities. Such reasoning, no matter how justifiable, does not work at present. On the contrary, it creates conflict with those who are unable or unwilling to respond. On one hand, those who are already weakened themselves respond defensively to your request because they are in no position to lend support and, on the other hand, those with the capacity to help respond hostilely because their motives cannot stand up to scrutiny. This is not, therefore, a time to act naively, seeking assistance from those who would have already offered help if they had the will or means to do so. This is, rather, a time to let our own work call out to those of similar spirit, thought, feelings, and vision. It is a time to let our work speak for itself. The best way to find support at this time is not to go looking for it—let others find us through our works. This is especially true if we wish to attract helping spirits or spiritual ancestors to guide and teach us. The best way to persuade others to come to our aid at this time is to persuade them of our sincerity. If you can push through this time with good intentions toward all, you will be joined by collaborators of the utmost worth.

SUMMARY | Avoid the temptation to seek out those who might help you in your endeavor, striving instead to produce something both beneficial and of the highest caliber. Likewise, avoid the temptation to seek the approval of others, striving instead for self-respect. Take joy in producing something you believe in and others will come to believe in your goal. Success falls to the patient at this time. Find joy in the daily repetition of the endeavor you have undertaken.

THE LINE CHANGES

1ST It would not be difficult for you to take advantage of people and enjoy a better lifestyle, yet you do not. Consider why you hold these ethics when so many do not—where does this sense of right and wrong come from? This lifestyle of good will and fair play eventually brings you an audience.

2ND Be careful here, for there are competing interests vying for your loyalty and neither are quite as they seem. Where the one that seems more relevant has a very dark side, the one that seems irrelevant is noble-hearted. Pause, look deeper, and decide slowly— you will live with this a long time.

3RD Among peers, there are negative leaders and positive leaders— while most people prefer to do good, it is more difficult to lead them that way in a group. Work in private, establishing bonds that will hold in public. Little by little you will sway them away from the negative leader.

4TH Do not merely avoid impropriety—avoid the appearance of impropriety. If you are not intensely aware of the importance of this at this time, you will create great ill for yourself. Everything must be aboveboard and above reproach—make no utterance or action without thinking it through twice.

5TH You are able to relax here, for you have found a place where your character and responsibilities are in accord. You are able to act ethically in all matters and you have others around you doing the same. Enact reforms now in order to prevent unscrupulous people from gaining power later.

6TH There can be no greater form of answering than to lead another person to self-sufficiency. The road of freedom requires its travelers to follow living principles, not dead doctrine. If you would teach, then listen; if you would listen, then watch; if you would watch, then close your eyes.

SEEING
AHEAD

IMAGE | A female warrior stops at a crossroads, determining which road she should take. The road to the right leads into mountains, behind which stands the sun. The road to the left crosses a level plain and leads toward the moon. The warrior, who carries all she needs for a long trip, kneels and consults the oracle by tossing kernels of corn. The oracle answers her question with a hummingbird, who points to the road toward the sun.

INTERPRETATION | This hexagram depicts the window of opportunity opening. The female warrior symbolizes the patience and acceptance to rest until the time comes to move. That she carries all she needs means that you are self-reliant and well-prepared for the journey ahead. That she pauses at a crossroads means that you stop to assess your situation and make plans for your next course of action even if doing so reawakens old fears, injuries, or resentments. The road to the sun beyond the mountain symbolizes a period of creativity that can only be reached by overcoming obstacles and difficulties. The road to the moon across the open plains is a symbol of future contentment and fulfillment that is within easy grasp. Consulting the oracle means that you trust the helping spirits to guide you toward your destiny. The hummingbird, who drinks only the nectar of beautiful flowers and can fly in any direction at will, is a symbol of the will power of a great warrior who returns from the house of the sun to encourage and inspire the living. Taken together, these symbols mean that your connection to the spirit world is strong, your vision is clear, your decisions are firm, and your actions inspired.

ACTION | The feminine half of the spirit warrior pauses in her journey, taking time to question her destiny about the road ahead: By stepping outside the flow of events and listening to the spirit of your lifetime, you ensure that all your decisions are in accord with the will of your guide. This is a time for stepping back from the immediacy of your emotions and being receptive to deeper, more sublime, urges welling up from the innermost sanctuary of *need*. Keeping in mind your dearest dreams and aspirations for this life, ask of the spirit helpers guidance in choosing the road that will lead you to that destination. From such a vantage point, survey the terrain ahead, noting in particular the landmarks by which you can keep your bearings and mark your progress. Lay out your plans now and map out your overall strategy for achieving your goal. Reminding yourself constantly that matters will not be this clear again for some time, take advantage of the time to project your will as far forward as possible. In this way, you arrive at decisions that fulfill a *need* greater than your own, decisions that multiply the *benefit* you receive into the lives of untold others.

INTENT | Sometimes the clear and easy path is the right road but this is not such a time. Your road leads beyond a steep mountain range that can be surmounted only by overcoming both inner and outer obstacles. But it is the radiance of solar light and its life-giving energy that calls you forward—it is the higher purpose given you by the creative forces that asserts itself anew. Dedicate yourself to reaching your life's destiny and you will establish the overall direction for the rest of your life. Don't shy away from hard work and don't settle for anything less than seeing matters through to the end. Be receptive to the presence of the helping spirits, for they bring the masculine half of the spirit warrior to bear on the moment: By being open to the insight and understanding of the spirit of the corn and to the courage and will power of the spirit of the hummingbird, you will be filled with the wisdom and strength to surmount every obstacle between you and your heart's desire.

SUMMARY | Set aside your hopes and fears, ignore the hopes and fears of others. Cultivate a more objective frame of mind, make the most of this time of clarity and insight. You are particularly attuned to the momentum of how things are developing at this time. Once you determine the proper course, do not hesitate to devise your plan of action and begin putting it into effect. Accept the challenge.

THE LINE CHANGES

1ST   If you allow being in a subordinate position to frustrate you, you will offend others and cut off aid you might otherwise receive. If you want recognition so badly, then this humbling is precisely what you need. Honor those around you and do not resent their air of superiority—time is your ally.

2ND   Occupying a lowly position can be a boon, for the wealthy and the powerful cannot trust anyone. Having little, you have no reason to distrust—the relationships you forge now will last a lifetime. Strive to be the equal of anyone in character and learning—follow your personal path.

3RD   Though the situation does not seem favorable, it is best to do nothing to change it—though you do not seem to be appreciated, it is best not to alter your demeanor. Circumstances will eventually bring your talents to the forefront. Continue honing your skills and contributing wherever asked.

4TH   Experience shows that it is often the second choice who succeeds when the first choice fails to work out. Tolerate no false pride or opportunism in yourself—respond with genuine gratitude now that your chance has come. You succeed now because you did not jump at lesser opportunities earlier.

5TH   There is nobility sometimes when figureheads fail. This is because it was their role all along to legitimize the transition from the old to the new and never to actually accomplish the task they ostensibly accepted. Play out your role with dignity and integrity—this is a joyous destiny.

6TH   When the two halves fly apart, the strong half sacrifices direct thought and action even as the adaptable half fails to nourish all it touches. You cannot produce any positive results under these conditions. Step aside gracefully and let others try—this was never your vision in the first place.

CONCENTRATING
ATTENTION

IMAGE | An ancient spirit, part man and part mountain, stands in the solitude of the wilderness. A storm gathers around his head and his hand rests on the ground out of which he rises. The creative energy of lightning strikes the crown of his head and the life-giving force of the sun perpetually rises behind a sacred mountain that is his heart.

INTERPRETATION | This hexagram depicts a time in which to attain great independence of spirit by disciplining your powers of concentration. The mountain is a symbol of wholeness, independence, and the unchanging. The man is a symbol of the training and refining of human nature. Taken together, these symbols mean that you focus your attention uninterruptedly upon the present moment. Lightning striking the head is symbolic of creative thought. Resting the hand on the fundamental is symbolic of concrete actions in accord with the underlying harmony of the world. Dawn within the heart of the mountain is symbolic of the eternal renewal of the infinite wilderness to be explored on the inner way. Taken together, these symbols mean that you fix your creative will upon actions that express the sacred nature of humanity's relationship with nature and the divine. When the sun-heart radiates *benefit*, then the will power of lightning-thought is translated into the actions of the hand-earth.

ACTION | The masculine half of the spirit warrior unites the intent of human nature with the intent of the mountain in order to slow time down to the present moment. Attending to matters not at hand dilutes our power and disperses our energy. Concentrating on matters not in the present time or place accelerates our experience of time by disrupting our continuity of awareness. The faster things are going on around us, the greater our need to concentrate fully on the matter at hand. When our concentration cannot be broken by either external or internal distractions, then we move at the pace of creation, wherein a single moment is long enough to experience the true potential of joy and a single lifetime is long enough to accomplish our purpose. Practice ignoring the trivial. Shut out habit thoughts and feelings and memories that have nothing to do with the moment at hand. Bear down on the single matter before you, with nothing else on your mind, and you will find that all the work you have been doing to refine your nature comes to the fore, expanding the moment into an unbroken landscape of sustained clarity and ample opportunities. Because you focus all your energy on opening up the potential locked within the moment, your accomplishments surpass your highest hopes.

INTENT | The time is ripe for advance. You can make great progress in your endeavor now if you don't dilute or waste your energy on needless and unjustifiable activities. Your capacity for pure and focused intent is great: There is nowhere but the present moment to be, there is nothing but the present action to do. The mountain waits, the storm comes: When your mind is calm and quiet and not preoccupied, then the energy to motivate and direct your efforts will have a place to dwell. Concentrate only on what you have decided to do—and do only those things that actively contribute to achieving your goal. Avoid planning your responses to what may occur. Instead, wait to see what unfolds and trust that your accumulated experience has prepared you to respond with great spontaneity and effectiveness. Resist making wasteful changes. Instead, conserve your energy by restricting your efforts to making just those changes that ennoble your motives and take you closer to completing what you have started.

SUMMARY | You must pay special attention now, concentrating on your endeavor without getting distracted by either inner or outer developments. Train your mind to interrupt your ordinary way of following every thought, emotion, and memory that captures your attention—if you continually bring your attention back to settle on the matter at hand, you will succeed in accomplishing your goals. Concentrate with your heart and your thinking will follow.

THE LINE CHANGES

1ST It is all well and good to set goals and make plans—if you can set them aside and live your life. It is all well and good to review your past and understand your history—if you can come back to your senses and live your life. You are where your concentration is—train it upon living your life.

2ND You would like to communicate with a superior but are held in check by gatekeepers. Not trickery, flattery, nor high-handed behavior will work. Instead of trying to bypass such people, convince them of the significance of your information—relationships work where scheming does not.

3RD What greater pleasure than to see wrong-doers corrected and the corrupted ousted. But fighting such battles makes it difficult to concentrate on your own affairs. Maintain the highest ethics and indulge no appearance of impropriety or the hunter will become the hunted.

4TH Changes are coming quickly and sometimes startlingly—do not take them personally. Turn this into a battle of principle and you will lose—pretend to go along with the changes and they will fade away. Concentrate on being grateful for the position you have and you will outlast this phase.

5TH Success is not only elusive—it is often difficult to recognize even when achieved. Go back and revisit your original goal and you will see you have exceeded your hopes. Those things not yet achieved were taken on later in the midst of the fray—celebrate victory before re-entering the battle.

6TH Concentrating on unrealistic goals becomes obsession—stop before idealism and principles create a negative backlash. Walk away from your daily concerns for a while and go visit new places you have wondered about. Concentrate on the daily concerns of new lands.

UNLOCKING
EVOLUTION

IMAGE | Ancient spirits, part human and part butterfly, emerge from cocoons that hang from the branches of a tree.

INTERPRETATION | This hexagram depicts the passage into a new and more ennobling stage of life. The human form symbolizes the body and its potential. The butterfly symbolizes the soul and its potential. The cocoon symbolizes a period of self-imposed isolation during which one undergoes transformation. The tree symbolizes continuity of the vision passing from the spirit ancestors to their living descendants. Taken together, these symbols mean that you turn inward to fulfill the timeless ideal of the evolving immortal. Of the features of the butterfly, the antennas symbolize senses beyond the five senses, the compound eyes symbolize looking at things from many different points of view, the proboscis symbolizes nourishing oneself only on the nectar of life, and the wings symbolize the capacity to rise above limitations. That many of these ancient spirits emerge from their cocoons at the same time means that you find spiritual companions on your journey. Taken together, these symbols mean that your own invisible progress is essential to the forging of the invisible community of spirit.

ACTION | The masculine and feminine halves of the spirit warrior—the human and butterfly forms, respectively—unite to form a more versatile and charismatic person. This is a time in which powerful forces, long dammed up within you, are finally released and allowed to come to expression. The higher potential you have long sensed approaching now falls within your reach. Remove yourself from your daily routines where you can and spend time by yourself in communion with nature and spirit. Turn your will inward, direct all your inner resources toward destroying every influence of the past that seeks to destroy your joy of life and sense of confidence. Consider the obstacles that have held you back, look at them from the perspective of the grandeur of the universe, reflect on their importance in the scheme of eternity. Sense the immortality of that which is beyond the senses, feel yourself an intrinsic part of the indivisible whole, see the world through the eyes of the ancestors' hopes and dreams for your life. Taking up the view that every lifetime is of the utmost consequence, you cease to act out of self-interest and rededicate yourself to another lifetime of bringing *benefit* to others. Allowing your heart to be touched by the ancestors' wishes for your happiness and well-being, you cease to be influenced by misfortunes and injustices and attempts to break your spirit. Taking wing amid the field of immortal spirit warriors, you learn to meet *need* with *benefit* everywhere it exists.

INTENT | The longer that beneficial intent is held in check by coercive and oppressive forces, the more momentous its release—when dark forces predominate, they eventually reveal their malicious intent, thereby creating among otherwise compliant people a constructive backlash. In this way, individuals who do not think of themselves as daring find themselves thrown forward into the very vanguard of change. Resist wrong-doing without doing wrong: Without attacking or defending, do not give an inch. This is a battle of wills whereby you will be transformed into a stronger and wiser warrior. This is an especially auspicious time to take up the discipline of creating yourself as you have always wished to be, rather than allowing others to define you. It is going to be exciting to the degree that you seek to take wing into the future—but unnerving to the degree that you seek the safety and security of the past. Above all, avoid becoming either restless or paralyzed by the pace of change: Have faith in the beneficial intent of metamorphosis going on within the cocoon. If you step back into your shadow-half and gaze unblinking upon the countenance of your light-half, this is a time in which all your inner obstacles are spontaneously changed into their opposites.

SUMMARY | You are entering a time of profound transformation. In order to advance, give up something in the past that has been holding you back. In order to give up something in the past, see yourself in the future. Consider what you will be like when your inner obstacles are no more. It is best to fashion a period of solitude in which you can crystallize your vision and solidify your intent.

THE LINE CHANGES

1ST Uncertainty is part of benefiting others. Does this person need words or food right now, am I helping someone who doesn't need help, can confrontation be as beneficial as encouragement? Just make all the mistakes you can helping others—when you run out of mistakes, keep helping.

2ND If you benefit others outside the home while ignoring those within, you will lose what you value most. If you strive to improve your social standing but ignore those closest to you, you will lose what you value most. Reserve the best and most of yourself to share with those dearest to you.

3RD The window of opportunity closes—there will not be another warning. The manner you have adopted with your peers and superiors threatens your position—continue like this and you bring long-term harm on yourself. Admit your mistake and become absolutely flexible and pleasant.

4TH Starting out easygoing and polite, you become assertive and confrontational—your frustration is justified. Those who hold the purse strings do not care about those below—you do what you must to help those you serve. Remember to temper the self-righteousness when things improve, though.

5TH When people reach levels of leadership for which they have no innate strengths, they are dependent on their advisors. Advisors, however, cannot be trusted to make great decisions—you must limit the scope of their concerns. Do not venture outside the range of your responsibilities.

6TH When people look up to you for guidance, there is no cause for celebration—it is a great sorrow that they do not yet trust their own greatness. Be trustworthy—guiding them to self-sufficiency is good, guiding them to depend on you is evil. With such care, all concerned reach the destination.

BELONGING
TOGETHER

IMAGE | A female warrior serves a simple but nutritious meal to her family. While her children wait to receive their portion, the steam rises to give form to the spirits of the ancestors, who are a vital part of the reunion.

INTERPRETATION | This hexagram represents the rituals of everyday life that bind people together in harmony and shared emotions. The female warrior here symbolizes the gentle, caring, and nurturing part of a person. The ancestors here symbolize the guardian spirits, whose love and concern for the living is immeasurable. The children here symbolize the living potential of the future, which blossoms fully only when it grows out of the rich tradition of loving families and ennobling homes. Taken together, these symbols mean that you actively seek to establish the kind of life in which you can nourish—and can be nourished by—all that is good and genuine dwelling in the past, present, and future. The food here symbolizes *benefit*, which always addresses *need* as if it were a hunger. The steam here symbolizes the spirit of cooked food and its smells, which forever anchor us to the shared blessing of mealtimes. The cooking fire here symbolizes the hearth, the center of the home, around which all belong. The bowls here symbolize the attitude of acceptance and gratitude with which great warriors acknowledge their dependence on the generosity of nature and spirit. Taken together, these symbols mean that you actively seek to create rituals of everyday life that fulfill and encourage those you call family—that you actively seek to create rituals of everyday life that consecrate and honor that which you call home.

ACTION | The feminine half of the spirit warrior gazes at the masculine half, offering him his bowl and welcoming him into the sacred space of the shared heart. Those who have been injured react by taking up a defensive posture, adopting the masculine force in order to protect the vulnerable potential in their care. Necessary and successful as such a strategy may have been, its time has passed and its effectiveness is coming to an end. Now is the time to break through your distrust, drop your defenses, and reclaim the sense of childlike innocence, openness, and safety that is your indisputable birthright.

Return to those rituals that bring you closer to whom and what you love, sharing them in order to keep them alive through others. Create new rituals of everyday life where they are needed, sharing them in order to give your vision and experience concrete form. Make the simple rituals of home life more sacred, more profound, and more symbolic by inviting more visits from your physical and spiritual ancestors. Keep in mind that upon your passing you will become one of the ancestors and that neither your love nor your concern for those with whom you belong will ever end. Such a perspective ensures that your connection to the ancestors remains strong and harmonious throughout your life.

INTENT | If you do not feel grateful for what you have, imagine what your life would be without it. If you do not feel appreciative for those around you, imagine what your life would be without them. Keep in mind the impermanence of everything you love, formalizing your heartfelt kinship through rituals by which all that you love might receive ever greater blessings. By not taking for granted the activities of everyday life, you recognize them as the very rituals of your spiritual practice. By not trivializing the activities of everyday life, you recognize them as the very exercises of the warrior's training. The simpler and more basic an activity is, the more essential and indispensable it is. The present generation must learn from the ancestors what it is that they miss most in order to make decisions that maintain the continuity of *benefit* running from the distant past to the far future. The basis of these simple things is the same basis from which all great creations spring: It is that which sustains life and spirit that brings people together in an ever-widening sense of meaningful communion, community, and culture. All of life, from the distant past to the far future, is bound together by the daily ritual of eating food. Opening our hearts to the ways in which we are not different is both the first and last step in the journey home.

SUMMARY | Do not forget those who count on you. Bring new allies into your circle, don't leave existing allies in order to join a new circle. It is essential to maintain the continuity of long-standing ritu-als and relationships. Fill your heart by pouring out all your loving-kindness daily. Surround yourself with love and acceptance by being loving and accepting. Be generous in thought, word, and deed.

THE LINE CHANGES

1ST Standards are established before you arrive on the scene. You are powerless until you know the opponent, yourself, and the surrounding circumstances intimately. Begin the long steep climb of experience and leave the work of correcting to others for now.

2ND A single word, a single act, when arising from innocence and good will, can tip the scales of a stagnant equilibrium into righting itself. It is not necessary to know the consequences ahead of time. All you need is faith in the cohesiveness of the nucleus.

3RD Do not just spend time discussing plans with your allies—make yourself the go-between with everyone in the opposition that you can reach. The opposing leadership cannot win if its soldiers fight half-heartedly. Convince the open-minded that their leaders are corrupted.

4TH In the middle of the river, people stop rowing—it is further and more difficult than they imagined. In its death throes, the old leadership puts up a final resistance of vicious delaying tactics—do not get unnerved. Deport yourself as if victory were already complete—start fulfilling your promises.

5TH When poor people win the lottery, they act like rich people overnight—when ordinary citizens become leaders, they act like leaders overnight. From the very beginning, conduct yourself like a great statesman, not a vicious general. Convert the old leadership—do not destroy them.

6TH New standards are established at the end—they may re-establish peace and stability but they cannot prevent future reversals. The momentum of reform cannot last—the new eventually becomes the old and corrupt people again assert themselves. The field must be plowed anew every spring.

RENEWING
DEVOTION

IMAGE | On the platform of a pyramid, male and female warriors greet the dawn with ceremonial fire, drum, and song. Out among the surrounding vegetation, a bird greets the dawn with two speech glyphs, one of which represents a flower and the other a song.

INTERPRETATION | The pyramid is a symbol of the sacred mountain at the center of all things and means that you are part of the collective work striving to mirror the handiwork of nature and the divine. The dawn is a symbol of the daily renewal of creation and greeting it with companions means that you have others with whom you share the song of your beliefs, the drumbeat of your passions, and the fire of your creativity. The surrounding vegetation is a symbol of the natural order and means that you are in harmony with the spirit of the world. The singing bird represents the winged, transcendent, essence of nature and means that you are free to spontaneously give voice to the pure joy of life. The flower and song glyphs represent the spirit warrior's philosophy of life and mean that you have the courage to confront the eventual passing of everything beautiful, as well as the dignity to honor each passing both before and after it occurs. Taken together, these symbols mean that your sincerity, trustworthiness, and persistence will bring you success, vindication, and contentment.

ACTION | The feminine and masculine halves of the spirit warrior unite to carry out past decisions. This is not the time for questioning the correctness of inner decisions such as your commitments to your beliefs, values, and viewpoints. Nor is it the time for second-guessing the wisdom of outer decisions such as your commitments to your duties, goals, and loved ones. It is, rather, the time for honoring your sense of honor—the time for renewing your devotion to the higher purpose guiding your life. Sometimes it is not a question of what we have faith in, but that our faith is strong and unshakeable. Likewise, it is not always a question of who or what we are faithful to, but that our faithfulness is pure and unbreakable. Your future circumstances are created out of today's actions, so set aside all thoughts of changing direction. Your future character is created out of today's motives, so set aside all self-doubt. You have taken a stand: Do not permit the opinions or actions of others to move you off center. Keep in mind that your decisions each have a symbolic value and represent part of your relationship with the whole of creation—by daily renewing your heartfelt devotion to acting with integrity, you will achieve the kind of consistency, firmness, and clarity that brings the highest *benefit* into your life and the lives of those around you.

INTENT | If we look for reasons to doubt the perfection of all creation, we will find them. Because the perfect nature with which we are born is overwhelmed by the collective self-doubt produced by human history, we come to doubt our own vision and are increasingly influenced by the prevailing viewpoint of the world as inhumane and, therefore, imperfect. It is this social indoctrination that creates an artificial viewpoint which obscures our original vision and, much as a mask covers the real face, creates in us an artificial sense of an imperfect nature. When we become aware that our true birthright is usurped when we are too young to defend the perfect nature we bring into the world, then we come to understand the old stories about the royal child who is hidden away until it comes of age and can reclaim its rightful place in the world. Once we recognize our true self as that part which was hidden in order to protect it until was strong enough to fend for itself, then we view the world through the eyes of our innate perfect nature and no longer remain blind to the perfection of all creation. Renewing their devotion to perfection every day, spirit warriors are tireless in their effort to remain aware that nature is spirit—and unfaltering in their decision to rejoice in the fact that they are a vital part of that perfect unity.

SUMMARY | Work to continually renew your heartfelt dedication to fulfilling the first ancestor's vision of the human spirit, especially when surrounded by others who lack the awareness and sensitivity to appreciate the presence of spirit everywhere. Stay true to your road and destination. At this time, influencing others is more proper than allowing them to influence you.

THE LINE CHANGES

1ST Take time to go on a journey by yourself. Just as the body needs food, the spirit needs new experiences—make it your intention to have meaningful experiences wherever you go. There may be lessons to learn from those you meet, but take on no companions on this journey.

2ND Even in the midst of a crowded city, don't leave your mountaintop hermitage—maintain the sovereignty of your personal evolution. Avoid being unduly influenced by others, no matter how close. The more you broaden and deepen yourself, the more you bring to your relationships.

3RD When your sensibilities are not finely attuned to the details of your surroundings, you will appear overconfident and awkward. In reality, you are simply missing cues and responding to the wrong things. Watch how others react to the same things and adapt their responses to your own.

4TH Exhibit humility regardless of your accomplishments, preferring to be content and serve those in need rather than to seek advancement and profit. Your peers may see this as you risking stagnation and obscurity but you can see their judgment is impaired in other ways. Stay on your path.

5TH The window of opportunity opens—all the different factors come together easily and in a timely manner. You are able to come to important decisions as easily as if they had already been made for you. All concerned reap real gain and escape unscathed the hidden liabilities.

6TH Look back at the period just passed and study it diligently, gleaning all the lessons you can from it. Do you feel more empowered or less empowered than before? What do you want to have continue, what do you want to have change?

GUIDING
FORCE

IMAGE | Above, a male warrior descends through twilight, reaching for the light of the daytime sun. Clinging to his back is his shadow, whom he carries with him. Below, his shadow reaches for a black sun as he walks through a bright place of scattered bones and approaches a living skeleton. In this place, the warrior clings to the back of his shadow, who carries him and guides him through the unfamiliar landscape.

INTERPRETATION | This hexagram depicts a journey into uncharted territory. The male warrior symbolizes the way of testing and training human nature that increases its versatility and fortitude. Descending through the twilight means that you take leave of the world of known and familiar experience. Reaching for the daytime sun means that you begin the journey believing that past experience can guide you through this new time. Carrying the shadow means that you have another half, a twin, that accompanies you everywhere, yet is so close and familiar to you that its presence is taken for granted. The shadow reaching for the black sun means that your other half is guided by a different, invisible, kind of light. Walking through a bright place of scattered bones means that your other half feels at home in the land of the ancestors, whose nocturnal sun turns the night to light. Approaching the living skeleton means that your other half visits with the spirit that does not die in order to return to the realm of the daytime sun with new knowledge and understanding. Being carried and guided by the shadow means that you increasingly trust the mysterious and hidden half of yourself to lead the way through unfamiliar and unforeseen experiences. Taken together, these symbols mean that you keep your bearings in even the most disorienting and confusing of times by believing in the strength, wisdom, and resourcefulness of your companion spirit.

ACTION | The masculine half of the spirit warrior follows the guide when passing through times of crisis and change. While our day-to-day practice involves honing our ability to make insightful judgments and far-sighted decisions, there are times when the trials facing us are greater than the strength and knowledge we have accumulated over the course of this lifetime. At times like this, it is necessary to change our orientation. Rather than pursuing our conscious decisions and goals, now is the time to follow up on coincidences and listen to our dreams. Facing in a new direction is not easy, however, since it means breaking habits of thought and feeling that have accrued over a long time. For this reason, it is necessary to rely on the transcendent intelligence of your spiritual ally, whose assistance is proof that selflessly benefiting others is the path of the evolving individual. By following your spiritual twin into new arenas at this time, you reach the goal you would have missed had you sought it directly.

INTENT | When a situation is beyond our control, our unconscious connection to spirit keeps us from getting lost. External change transforms us internally—and because change is constant, we are in a perpetual state of transformation. There is, however, another part of us that never changes, an essence that leaves the body just as it entered it. Difficult to find when sought, it emerges spontaneously when most needed: We look through our guide's eyes when we see the unchanging harmony underlying the world of appearances. Independent of the social and cultural upbringing that determines so much of how we experience the world and respond to it, this essence is like a spark of the spiritual sun—arrived here from the source of light and life and love, it guides us through dark times, comforts us in fearful times, and draws us closer in solitary times. External change transforms us internally—and because every transformation forces us to consider leaving some part of ourselves behind, every change reminds us of the great leave-taking at death. It is our spirit ally who maintains contact with the spirit world, providing us with the means to experience the wisdom and love of our predecessors. The closer we move to leaving this realm and entering the realm of the ancestors, the better we understand the importance of the two realms being governed by the same vision of universal peace and well-being. We feel with the twin's heart when we know that the realm of the living and the realm of the dead are in reality one and the same realm of spirit.

SUMMARY | Because you maintain great inner flexibility and adaptability, you pass through even the most trying and confusing of times without losing your bearings. Trust your hidden potential to come forth when needed and help solve problems beyond your conscious ability. Do not place limits on the limitless, do not lose touch with your own miraculous nature. Step into the flow of spirit's intention and it will carry you into the ecstatic life.

THE LINE CHANGES

1ST There are those close to you whose contribution will make the endeavor successful. The kindness you have shown them in the past creates an atmosphere of trust and willing sacrifices. The values you hold in common make possible the benefit you both will enjoy from this collaboration.

2ND The window of opportunity opens—the situation is complex and the path to the goal intricate. But you are in the right place at the right time with the right skills and the right allies. Move now with the utmost confidence, scooping up others' terrain like chess pieces.

3RD This is a minor setback—given the circumstances, you should have seen it coming. Take it in stride, demonstrating an inner sense of self that is impervious to external failure, defeat, or rejection. Show your mettle and the next break will fall your way.

4TH Things are stable and going well but do not take them for granted. Maintain good relations with those around you, treating each with politeness and warm-hearted affection. Do not sow the seeds of your own hardships by treating others poorly.

5TH Your reputation for competence, judiciousness, and beneficial action spreads. Others will come of their own accord to form partnerships. Be gracious to all but accept only those whose character and resources actually advance the cause.

6TH Things have run their course—hand over the reins to others and move on to other less trying matters. Savor the joy of having had such a glorious journey and do not regret that it comes to an end. Hanging on at this point would be humiliating and threaten much of what you have created.

RESOLVING
PARADOX

IMAGE | Two intertwining serpents, one of water and one of fire, unite. Their tails braid into a rope that forms the umbilical cord of a gestating infant. From their union there also comes a bifurcated tongue that forms a single speech glyph representing a flower and song of jade.

INTERPRETATION | This hexagram depicts the creative power that is released by the marriage of opposites. The intertwining serpents symbolize the duality of the two great creative forces of the universe, whose union forms the mystery that is the core of every individual creation. The tail symbolizes that which follows, or results from, something. The rope symbolizes that which ties together or which provides continuity. The umbilical cord symbolizes hidden nourishment or an invisible wellspring. The gestating infant symbolizes both the impending birth of something new and the loving care it requires if it is to develop fully. Taken together, these symbols mean that you protect a new creation whose connection with the unseen forces provides continuity between the past and the future. The bifurcated tongue symbolizes that which appears to be two but is in reality one. The single speech glyph of a jade flower and song symbolizes the single voice of philosophy, art, wisdom, and compassion with which the great duality speaks. Taken together, they mean that your thoughts, words, and actions increasingly give expression to the bittersweet experience of being born into a perfect world which you must inevitably leave.

ACTION | The masculine and feminine halves of the spirit warrior are but one aspect of the universal duality making up the unitary nature of the world. Most of our preventable difficulties in life arise from a failure to integrate our own personal halves with their universal counterparts, symbolized by fire and water. Preventing such difficulties from arising, therefore, is a matter of internal action: Aligning the masculine half of the spirit warrior with the beneficial direct action of universal fire and the feminine half of the spirit warrior with the beneficial flexible nurturing of universal water, we find the rhythm of the life-giving and life-sustaining forces and move with them effortlessly through the world of change. In this way, we recognize that the masculine half of the spirit warrior is not aligned properly when we experience frustration and aggressiveness—and that it is brought back into alignment by reverting to the beneficial flexible nurturing of universal water. Likewise, we recognize that the feminine half of the spirit warrior is not aligned properly when we experience apathy and desperation—and that it is brought back into alignment by reverting to the purposeful direct action of universal fire. Using the irrational forces to refine and cultivate the rational forces in this way is like gestating an immortal child in the womb of your spirit.

INTENT | When two opposing needs, such as the need for security and the need for freedom, are equally strong at the same time, conflicts arise that are too often met by sacrificing one of the needs. Such solutions do not work and, eventually, prove harmful. Placing the need for security above the need for freedom, for example, does not simply create a prison—eventually, it makes its prisoners more insecure than ever. Likewise, placing the need for freedom above the need for security does not simply create vulnerability—eventually, it makes its homeless more dependent than ever. Paradoxes cannot be resolved by choosing one need, belief, value, desire, or ideology over its opposite. On the contrary, such paired opposites are in reality complements to one another: They mutually fulfill each other's lack, together making a whole whose unity they serve. Aligning the need for security with universal fire and the need for freedom with universal water, for example, demonstrates that an over-zealous pursuit of security leads to aggressiveness and an over-zealous pursuit of freedom leads to apathy. This aggressiveness is an illness of over-zealous fire that its complement, beneficial flexible nurturing, remedies. Likewise, this apathy is an illness of over-zealous water that its complement, purposeful direct action, remedies. Using the rational forces to balance and harmonize the irrational forces in this way is like a sacred marriage of two perfectly matched halves of an unimaginable whole.

SUMMARY | Two equally strong needs appear to oppose one another, tempting you to choose one over the other. This is not the time for a decision—wait instead for an opportunity that allows you to join these needs into a third, more comprehensive, goal. Continually balance each negative extreme with its positive opposite and frustration will give way to greater insights and creativity. Seek out new experiences that evoke unexpected and unfamiliar feelings and ideas. Remain unnerved by change.

THE LINE CHANGES

1ST   When paradox is the rule, people often find themselves quarreling over the dividing of the spoils before the last battle is fought. Such disunity and flagrant self-interest bode ill—establish a unity of purpose and sense of self-sacrifice now or find new allies. The first step augurs the last.

2ND   When paradox is the rule, you must rely on your partners and not doubt their motives or capabilities. Likewise, do not make your allies doubt your own sincerity or confidence—you must all pull together with a single will. Great rewards await the stout of heart and stalwart companions.

3RD   When paradox is the rule, people often find themselves trying to rush ahead without first completing the task at hand. Such amateurishness and flagrant impropriety bode ill—establish a method of review and evaluation now or accept defeat. The old ways cannot lead to the new way.

4TH   When paradox is the rule, you must accept challenging tasks and strive tenaciously until they are completed. You may not feel prepared but trust that you will rise to the occasion—you do not know your potential until you have the chance to exercise it. This is the road of the ecstatic life.

5TH   When paradox is the rule, people often find themselves depending on supporters who are stronger and more experienced than they. This bodes ill if you are not of the same mind—establish a way for advice to be rendered without confusing your respective roles. Do not grow apart.

6TH   When paradox is the rule, you must be able to remain calm in the midst of activity and sober in the midst of excitement. Do not get carried away by the celebratory atmosphere—reaching the further shore is just the first step of a new journey. It is pleasant to rejoice—now, back to work.

CELEBRATING
PASSAGE

IMAGE | Four female warriors conduct a ritual of rejoicing, dancing in a circle amid the waves of the ocean. Above them, the moon traverses the night, passing through its four phases.

INTERPRETATION | The four warriors symbolize the four stages of life—the child, the youth, the adult, and the elder. That they dance in a circle symbolizes the passage of every life through each of these stages and into the next generation. That they make a ritual of rejoicing symbolizes the spirit warrior's attitude toward the world and its gift of sacred life. That they dance in the waves of the sea shows that rejoicing transports them beyond the shore of reason and immerses them in the oceanic experience of the oneness of all creation. The moon, as the light that illumines the mystery of night, is a symbol of the feminine force governing the tides of the sea and the cycles of fertility. Taken together, these symbols mean that you are, in every stage of life and every activity, celebration itself.

ACTION | The feminine half of the spirit warrior dares to feel the loving-kindness cradling the whole of the world in its arms. Everyday life is highly ritualized: Arising at the same time, performing the same tasks in the same order, eating the same types of food, feeling the same emotions, thinking the same thoughts, we ritualize our lives to satisfy little more than our comfort and habits. By converting what we do unconsciously into consciously created rituals that recognize and honor the transitions of our everyday lives, however, we can use our mundane habits to train ourselves to rejoice in the everyday passage of life. Transitions are those passages between endings and new beginnings: One stage of life ends and another begins; the waxing moon ends with the full moon and the waning moon begins; the night ends at dawn and a new day begins; one feeling ends and a new one begins; one way of life ends and a new one begins. Whether in solitude or with companions, whether marking the great milestones of life or the minutest of transitions, this is a time for creating rituals that recognize and honor the sacred nature of the knot that ties the rope of metamorphosis into the great circle of unending renewal.

INTENT | It is a time for the masculine half of the spirit warrior to set aside goals and follow the feminine half back to where all hearts meet. Without unshakeable faith in the benevolence of the unseen forces, life can be misconstrued as a random series of meaningless events. Without unshakeable faith in the spiritual path ahead, progress can be misconstrued as achieving personal gain at the expense of others. Without unshakeable faith in the indestructibility of spirit, death can be misconstrued as a terrifying extinction of awareness. Confronting our doubts, we find where the path of life diverges, one road leading to sorrow and the other to joy. Confronting the limits of reason, we find that the intellect can never have all doubts settled by reason alone, so we turn to the heart to guide us back home. Confronting our fears, we find where the path of spirit diverges, one road leading to aloneness and the other to communion. When we see the world as created by love, sustained by love, and occupied by love, then the greater part of our work becomes the tearing down of those barriers around our hearts that keep us from feeling the presence of that love. By rejoicing in the loving-kindness that ties endings to new beginnings, we train the masculine half of the spirit warrior to follow the path of celebration. By stepping away from the shore of materialism and immersing ourselves in the ritual of life that is being re-enacted every moment of creation, we create our own rituals that help us find our place in the world, connecting us to the unending cycles of life, spirit, and creation.

SUMMARY | Recognize your good fortune. Find cause for rejoicing every moment. Sustain your good will by reminding yourself constantly that all this is passing, that even hardship and grief help make up the fabric of this lifetime that you celebrate. Bless the world with your adoration, do not grow numb to the wonder of creation. Seek the divine within every moment. Share your road with companions.

THE LINE CHANGES

1ST   You have a sense of high purpose and of a more harmonious way
of life but those around you are still enamored with the status
quo. If you move them by force of argument or personality, they
soon return to their old ways, now feeling shamed. Go ahead by
yourself—they will catch up later.

2ND   You have maintained an ethical intent for a long time, so you are
fully deserving of the relationship you seek. You have maintained
a sincere heart for a long time, so you are fully deserving of the
trust you solicit. Focus on shared hopes and fears to cement the
relationship.

3RD   You have little in common with your peers and only the loosest
connection to those above. Seeing the impasse developing, you
approach those above in order to learn from their experience.
Though you are not yet adept at calling others together, you learn
how from those who are.

4TH   You have planted strong seeds and will reap a great harvest—people will hear your call and respond favorably. Base your words
and actions on established precedents in order to gain the confidence of those above and below. Stay vigilant—avoid any backlash your work could provoke.

5TH   You have risen to a position of prominence but that alone does
not entitle you to respect—others are equally qualified, so you
must demonstrate your exceptional abilities. Do not worry—
the greater the skepticism, the greater the conviction when per-
suaded. In time, you will win them all over.

6TH   You have spiritual pursuits you must not ignore. As with the
spirit guides you call to you, mourners will one day encircle your
death bed and all you worked for will slip away. Keep one eye
trained on the far shore—what senses will you go by when this
body is gone?

ENTERING
SERVICE

IMAGE | An old man steps onto a long road that winds up a mountain, at the summit of which a plant grows. He carries everything he needs for a long journey. Under his arm, he carries a painted book of healing plants, opened to a plant matching the one on the summit before him. His walking stick is in the form of a serpent.

INTERPRETATION | The old man represents wisdom gained through experience and means you are more concerned with bringing *benefit* to others than you are with receiving recognition for your efforts. The plant at the mountain's summit represents a distant goal and the long road winding up to it symbolizes the many twists and turns facing you on your lengthy journey. That he carries everything he needs for a long journey means that you have anticipated hardship and prepared for it ahead of time. The painted book of medicinal plants symbolizes the knowledge of the ancestors that is as relevant in the present as it was in the past. That the book is opened to a painting matching the plant living atop the summit means that your goal is part of the living tradition of the old ones. The walking stick in the form of a serpent symbolizes a helping spirit who knows the way on this winding and convoluted path. Taken together, these symbols mean that you initiate a new and fuller realization of your potential by materially helping others obtain what they most need.

ACTION | The masculine half of the spirit warrior undertakes an arduous journey in order to alleviate the *need* of others. The quest to find *benefit* is a noble calling but one to be undertaken only when we are willing to accept the trials by which we acquire practical knowledge and ready to accept the tribulations by which we learn self-sacrifice. Because experience has taught you that serving others is a nobler pursuit than serving yourself, you do not hesitate to take up this next leg of your journey. Because it will be a long and difficult endeavor, you set your determination to see matters through to the end. Because you cannot always count on others to make the hard parts of the journey easier, you make yourself self-reliant, flexible, and strong. Because others lack consistency of vision and become periodically fascinated by new ideas, you study on your own and incorporate time-proven methods into your approach. Because you strive to realize the highest vision, you pay close and constant attention to your spirit guide, who steers you clear of the pitfalls on the road of service.

INTENT | Observe those who profess to be pursuing a goal similar to your own. Distinguish between those motivated by selflessness and those motivated by self-interest, between those content to fulfill their duty to others and those striving for advancement and recognition. Learn from the ambitious that ulterior motives poison *benefit*. Learn from the selfless that pure intentions nourish *benefit*. By weeding out unnatural feelings of being taken advantage of, you cultivate your innate garden of sincerity, devotion, and generosity. By observing those who habitually exhibit cynicism and self-righteous indignation, you learn that poison eventually poisons the one who produces it. By observing the incorruptible benevolence of your helping spirit, you learn that enduring noble-heartedness is itself the road by which you yourself become *benefit*. Sow your seeds of intent in the timeless, that others might receive *benefit* in time.

SUMMARY | Do not forget that you have undertaken a difficult road in order to benefit others. Watch your reactions carefully, making sure that you harbor neither resentment toward those you serve nor distrust of those with whom you serve. Continue to focus on the ideal of your goal, allow your journey to ennoble you. Do not listen to voices that sow dissension or dissatisfaction in your heart.

THE LINE CHANGES

1ST Just because you can do something doesn't mean you should—to humble others is seldom wise. Keep your thoughts to yourself and use your talents to build others up. These matters are not essential to you, so stop being so invested in them and help others around you succeed.

2ND Just because the rule worked once doesn't mean it will work again—conditions have changed and you must change with them. You are being too cautious and acting as if you had no confidence. Envision how this partnership fits with your long-range goals and then act.

3RD Just because one thing doesn't work doesn't mean its opposite will—you must not swing from extreme to extreme. Go no higher for a while—you must master this level before advancing again. Adopt a permanent demeanor of having just finished a full meal—be without any hunger.

4TH Just because you have good ideas doesn't mean others haven't thought of them earlier—look for those who are already working toward your goal. These are the people to learn from and align with. Think no further than adding your energy to their momentum.

5TH Just because the present is easy doesn't mean the future will be—what makes great leaders is their ability to adapt to future conditions. Now is the time to temper extravagance, pay off debts, and invest in promising ideas. This is the road to redoubling your future blessings.

6TH People are malleable but cannot be oppressed indefinitely—clamping down too tight makes them question authority. Once they begin looking into their own authority, their spirits can no longer be molded to another's will. Step forward to meet their material needs and you will win their loyalty.

CULTIVATING
CHARACTER

IMAGE | A female warrior hoes a cornfield amid inhospitable mountains. She has no one to help her, yet her crop is strong and vital.

INTERPRETATION | This hexagram depicts the inevitable success of those who develop an undefeatable will to make their own place in the world. The female warrior symbolizes the way of nurturing and encouraging human nature that increases its sensitivity and loving-kindness. That she cultivates the cornfield means that you nurture something that will nurture you, especially by resolutely weeding out any influences that might keep your efforts from bearing fruit. That she lives and works amid inhospitable mountains means that you find a way to adapt to even the most difficult circumstances. Raising a strong crop without help means that you succeed because you do not rely on others to do your hard work for you. Taken together, these symbols mean that you use your circumstances to refine your inner nature.

ACTION | The feminine half of the spirit warrior uses external hardship to cultivate profound inner strength and flexibility. What is essential here is that energy not be wasted on futile actions, thoughts, or feelings. It is especially important that frustration and impatience be uprooted at every turn. When external progress is blocked, it is time to concentrate on inner progress. By focusing on the opportunity that is present rather than those that are absent, you sustain the attitude of appreciation and devotion that leads to a heart and mind filled with virtue. Set aside external goals for a time and concentrate on nourishing your obstacles: Treat them with respect, respond to them with concern, grow something productive where it seems nothing can grow. Let difficulties be like fire: Feed them with wood so that their flames might burn off all your impurities. By being grateful for your ordeals, you do away with self-pity and self-indulgence. By turning outer oppression into an inner discipline, you create a source of joy in the midst of deprivation. By transforming outer *need* into inner *benefit*, you find the source of spiritual power and wealth. By using obstacles as a whetstone upon which to hone your character, you conscientiously transform your habitual reactions into virtuous ones, achieving thereby greater readiness for the opportunities ahead.

INTENT | You cannot feign sincerity and humility to yourself. The feminine half of the spirit warrior concentrates on fulfilling responsibilities without any unworthy thoughts, feelings, or actions. By allowing hardship to move you closer to spirit, you let go of the tendency to take things personally, thereby quelling both anger and righteous indignation. Increasing the positive feminine half while decreasing the negative masculine half, the spirit warrior cultivates what is nourishing and weeds out the rest—and that which is most nourishing is sincerity, for that is the fertile ground out of which inner worthiness grows. Sincerely seeking to refine your character while responding to difficulties with generous humility, you make yourself so adaptable that you can thrive in any surroundings.

SUMMARY | Repeating the same act over and over, you are making yourself a worthy instrument of life by wearing away all that is petty and self-destructive. Though the outer reward may not be substantial, your diligence polishes your spirit into a priceless jewel. Use routine and repetition to build inner skills that can carry over into any field of endeavor. The momentum is with you.

THE LINE CHANGES

1ST   You push yourself too hard too soon—this is not the way to build up endurance and confidence. If you continue in this vein, you will actually defeat your own purpose at the very beginning. Back off and wait a while before starting over again.

2ND   Your progress is interrupted by a sudden crisis in the life of someone close to you. It is only fitting that you set aside your routine and spend time with all concerned. This is a time for unity and support, not individual effort—clear your mind of your training and focus on those around you.

3RD   You are too eager to prove yourself—you must not yet challenge those with more experience and skill than yourself. Getting ready for such a contest requires long, arduous, repetitive practice. Many have talent, few transmute it into greatness—true greatness is born of great stubbornness.

4TH   Training is always much more mental than physical—your nature is so rash and impatient that it must be tempered by calm judgment. Stop looking ahead, stop imagining scenes of success, stop exciting your emotions. Train mentally and you will achieve more than you imagine.

5TH   The greatest impediment to your training is the desire to prove yourself—this is a reflection of your not believing in your own greatness. Your efforts have carried you far by now, though, and you are able to pull this weed up by its roots. In this way you defeat the greatest opponent you ever face.

6TH   Self-imposed hardship is like voluntarily setting limits on spending in order to save for something important. Continue cultivating spiritual understanding and virtue. The road of freedom beckons you to rejoin your old companions.

SHARING
MEMORY

IMAGE | A male warrior conducts a ritual inside a fire-lit cave. He chants and drums in order to invoke the spirits of the ancients to come and speak to him. A jar of water sits beside the heated heart-shaped stone. When its water is thrown onto the stone it hisses loudly and calls to the ancients, who appear in the rising steam.

INTERPRETATION | The cave symbolizes both the womb and the tomb, a place for honoring the sacred union of birth and death. The firelight in the cave is symbolic of the light of intelligence that can penetrate the darkness of the great mystery. The male warrior conducting a ritual symbolizes an inner journey to gain answers to questions in order to restore an imbalance to its proper harmony. Chanting and drumming symbolize the ancients' natural response to the glory of the first dawn. Asking the ancestors' spirits to communicate symbolizes a willingness to quiet the everyday mind and listen to the wisdom and loving-kindness of those who came before us and count on us to fulfill their vision. The jar of water symbolizes the womb, the moon, and the fertility of the feminine creative force. The stone in the shape of a heart symbolizes that which animates and illuminates the memory. Throwing water onto the heated stone represents the marriage of universal opposites and the resulting steam symbolizes the creative power to ask for and receive a vision of the living memory of the ancients. Taken together, these symbols mean that you sit in council with the ancestors when alone.

ACTION | The masculine half of the spirit warrior journeys inward to reconcile the past and future. When we consider our own death and the goals that might motivate our spirits then, it is clear that we should try to help the living avoid unnecessary mistakes in order to make the world a more harmonious and beneficial home for our collective descendants. In this regard we are no different than our collective ancestors, who stand vigil at the doorway of the One Spirit, patiently awaiting any sincere request for help. Finding that doorway is not difficult for those who approach with a genuine seriousness of purpose: Search your heart to ensure it contains no ulterior motive and then create a heartfelt ritual that focuses all your attention and emotion on the *need* at hand. Such single-minded concentration frees your everyday mind from distractions, enabling you to hear the old ones answering your question. Whether you seek *benefit* for yourself or others, the knowledge you receive from the collective memory of the One Spirit enables you to formulate a course of action that recovers whatever had been lost, hidden, or stolen.

INTENT | It is in the heart that intention dwells and it is through the heart that intention speaks: If our heart is true, then the spirit allies do not hesitate to answer our call for help in breaking through an impasse. It is in the heart that ritual dwells and it is through the heart that ritual speaks: If our heart is dignified, then the spirit allies do not hesitate to let us take part in their ritual of collective remembering. It is in the heart that spiritual medicine dwells and it is through the heart that spiritual medicine speaks: If our heart is reverential, then the spirit allies do not hesitate to help us recognize the essence of even those things wholly unfamiliar to us. True, dignified, and reverential, the spirit warrior's heart is a cave wherein the spirits of the ancestors and the spirits of the descendants reunite in the communion of shared remembering.

SUMMARY | Quiet the inner voice that chatters constantly about your life. Listen to the drumbeat of your heart, allow your surroundings to purify you. Make yourself into a cave where the voices of the wise and loving ancestors still echo. Hear the inner voice that speaks to you of the right path of life, the right conduct in life, and the right relationships in life—this voice is the memory of the common good.

THE LINE CHANGES

1ST Sight-seeing does not a pilgrimage make—if you aspire only to petty things, you will never be part of anything great. Everywhere, people trivialize their hearts and minds—do not follow that flickering flame. Orient yourself to the unmoving polestar of the unchanging way.

2ND If you do not have a companion before you set out, you will meet one on the road right away. This proves to be a complex relationship, filled with many surprises, but one that is mutually beneficial. Be understanding—even boon companions are forever strangers and must eventually part ways.

3RD Just because you are only stopping over does not mean you treat your peers as inferior. If you do not study and respect the culture of those around you, you will find yourself alone and destitute. Adopt the customs of the time and you will pass unimpeded along each step of your pilgrimage.

4TH You've become so adaptable that your skills are recognized and your needs met. What begins as a stop-over becomes a trap of comfort and ease—you must plan your disentanglement so that those who trust you are not harmed. As long as you stay, keep in mind that this, too, is the pilgrimage.

5TH The window of opportunity opens—you encounter the sacred at every station of the pilgrimage. As you become the pilgrimage itself and cannot remember a time before it, you are reunited with old traveling companions. This is the road of the ecstatic life.

6TH The rider must care for the horse, letting it water, eat, and rest as needed—otherwise, the horse dies before the rider knows it is exhausted. To understand your mount is to have a meaningful and memorable journey. To lose your steed through carelessness is to cut the journey short.

WIELDING
PASSION

IMAGE | A naked female warrior rides a great serpent across the sky. Even as she points to the open sky where there are no clouds, the serpent carries her there.

INTERPRETATION | This hexagram depicts the creative power of the passions. The serpent symbolizes the driving force of the instincts and desires. The female warrior symbolizes the feminine creative force, who conceives in order to nurture and sustain what is valuable. Being naked means that nothing stands between you and the world. The clouds symbolize the obscuring of the sun's light and the concealing of clarity, beauty, and joy. Riding the serpent into the open sky means that you liberate your inner nature in order to experience firsthand the bliss of being fully alive. Taken together, these symbols mean that you dare to incorporate the full spectrum of human experience into a rich and rewarding lifetime.

ACTION | The feminine half of the spirit warrior channels passion into constructive acts of *benefit*. Those who encourage and inspire others must themselves find encouragement and inspiration. When we deny ourselves the pleasure, excitement, and enthusiasm engendered by new and intoxicating experiences, we find the well of creativity, generosity, and loving-kindness drying up, making it increasingly difficult to contribute to others' lives in a meaningful way. Because it is so easy to make mistakes when freeing the passions, much of our upbringing stresses the control and suppression of these powerful inner forces. Likewise, because it is so easy to be manipulated by those appealing to our passions, we learn to distrust and discount these life-affirming forces. When the feminine half of the spirit warrior encounters inner stagnation and apathy, it is because the source of personal fulfillment has been dammed up too long. This is a time for re-entering the sense of adventure that comes with an awareness of just how precious each fleeting moment truly is. Living with passion without being ruled by it, you avoid self-indulgence and self-centeredness by finding constructive outlets for the spirited energy you awaken. Because the passions are inherently life-affirming, they are by their very nature creative. For this reason, they do not need to be directed or controlled in order to be constructive. Rather, they find expression through us when we remain constant in our commitment to marshal all our inner resources toward preserving and protecting that which is most valuable.

INTENT | When a bonfire is kindled, it produces heat. Similarly, when the passions are aroused, they produce energy. When the heat of a fire is applied constructively, it can cook food or fire pottery or convert water to steam. Similarly, when the energy of the passions is applied constructively, it can create art or overcome oppression or convert weakness into strength. When fire is not tended properly, it either burns too hot or dies out. Similarly, when the passions are not attended to properly, they either result in compulsiveness or numbness. For this reason, it is essential to achieve a balance between a sense of purposefulness and a sense of playfulness. Just as too much seriousness and not enough playfulness is like having responsibility without freedom, too much playfulness without enough seriousness is like having freedom without responsibility. Balancing your responsibility to truly nourish others with your freedom to be truly nourished, you convert your passions into good works and they convert you into joy.

SUMMARY | Tame the masculine creative force with loving-kindness, animate the feminine creative force with freedom. Unite their forces within yourself and each of your works will be like a force of nature. Channel your passions into constructive and beneficial acts instead of trying to control or suppress them. Dare to explore new horizons and develop new avenues for self-expression.

THE LINE CHANGES

1ST   Roles and relationships can be entered into with such sincerity and integrity that fulfilling them may become the be-all and end-all of daily life, trapping us in an identity that represses our true nature. Break free of every mold without harming others. Keep the child's excitement for life ever alive.

2ND   Customs and values change, not just over the course of centuries but even within our lifetime. Do not allow yourself to be domesticated and then regret your timidity late in life. Find others who are light-hearted and creative—this is the path of the ecstatic life.

3RD   The window of opportunity closes—there will not be another warning. When people exaggerate their strength, overestimate their cunning, and underestimate their opposition, they cannot succeed. The wrong passions at the wrong time expressed in the wrong way lead to disaster.

4TH   When your personal ethics differ from those of your peers, make sure they are based on firsthand knowledge and not on abstract principles or ideology. Only then give voice to your growing concerns. Though this brings conflict, it will also draw superior allies—do not adopt others' timidity.

5TH   The outsiders who misunderstand your endeavor continue to successfully obstruct your progress. Even those close to you begin supporting some of their ideas. After some initial anger, you listen more receptively—though divisions remain, you see your own one-sidedness helped spur theirs.

6TH   You have an epiphany—those you thought were trying to harm you were merely trying to get you back to the table. They need your strength and resources just as you need their support and cooperation. You must make the first move toward reconciliation and normalization.

REVEALING
KNOWLEDGE

IMAGE | While picking up stones with which to build his home, a male warrior unearths a great treasure from the past. The ancient pyramid buried beneath his field holds precious artifacts and creations from the time of the ancestors.

INTERPRETATION | This hexagram depicts the attitude of remaining alert to the ever-present potential for new discoveries. The male warrior symbolizes the masculine creative force, who conceives in order to explore the unknown and uncover the hidden. Clearing the field of stones and using them to build a house means that you turn what others see as useless into a valuable resource. Building a home atop the buried pyramid means that you build your future on the foundation established by the ancestors. Unearthing a treasure trove of the ancestors' creations in the midst of daily activities means that you experience the extraordinary power of the creative spirit in the midst of ordinary experiences. Taken together, these symbols mean that you are increasingly aware of the unseen forces at work on the transformation of the visible.

ACTION | The masculine half of the spirit warrior roots out preconceptions in order to look at every moment with new eyes. Of all the different kinds of discoveries, the most profound are those that present us with a new and more vital sense of the meaningfulness present in our immediate surroundings. Because being at peace with the world and being content with our life is essential to feeling complete and fulfilled, we long to catch sight of the divine as it continues its work of creation. Every time we see the world for the first time, we experience the open heart and open mind as one and are touched to the very core by the loving rays of the perpetual dawn of creation. This is a time for canceling out thoughts of goals or hopes or fears, replacing your preconceptions with a sincere willingness to see the hidden perfection right before your eyes. Likewise, root out any feelings of unworthiness or doubt by purifying the heart of any feelings of envy, resentment, or anger, so that it stands ready to be filled with feelings of relief, joy, and homecoming. Stay vigilant and you will not miss a single opportunity to immerse yourself in the momentous.

INTENT | When you are entrusted with secrets, do not be in a hurry to share them with others. Consider the time and effort you have expended to become trusted—can others gain from your firsthand knowledge if they haven't had the experience itself? Consider the unexpected and unforeseen nature of the experience—can others gain from your description if the experience cannot be reproduced at will? Consider how your understanding and expression of your experiences always improve over time—can others make lasting gains based on the emotionality of your first impressions? Spend time integrating your vision with everyday life, finding its deeper meanings further and further within the details of ordinary experience. Translate your vision into action, responding to all you encounter with growing consistency and congruity, methodically training your thoughts and emotions and words and deeds to reflect the ancient and secret light you keep in your heart.

SUMMARY | Look more closely at ordinary everyday events and ask yourself what deeper meaning lies concealed within them. Look at the present as being built upon the hidden pyramid of the past and ask yourself what eternal meanings lie concealed just below the surface of your habits and routines. In the midst of your work, a whole new world opens up to you. Follow your sense of wonder.

THE LINE CHANGES

1ST   Nature reveals knowledge by analogy—you are attuned to the spirit of the land and sky. From the mountains and waters, from the weather and stars, from the plants and seasons, you gain insight into and wisdom about the cycle of creation. You feel more loved by the world every day.

2ND   Nature reveals knowledge by analogy—you are attuned to the spirit of the animal kingdom. From the intelligence and emotions of animals everywhere, you gain insight into and wisdom about the perfection of life. You grow in compassion and courage every day.

3RD   Human nature reveals knowledge by intimacy—you are attuned to the spirit of children. From the open-hearted and open-minded nature of children, you gain insight into and wisdom about the way potential can be nurtured or hindered. Your potential for joy increases every day.

4TH   Human nature reveals knowledge by intimacy—you are attuned to the spirit of companionship. From close and ongoing contact with loved ones, you gain insight into and wisdom about the fragility and resiliency of relationships. You are more trusting and trustworthy every day.

5TH   Spirit reveals knowledge by surprise—you are attuned to the spirit of language. From close observation of the way language shapes perception and reaction, you gain insight into and wisdom about the limits of language. Your sensitivity to the world beyond definitions increases every day.

6TH   Spirit reveals knowledge by surprise—you are attuned to the spirit of dreams. From close observation of the way dreams change perceptions and reactions, you gain insight into and wisdom about the limits of the senses. Your sensitivity to the invisible and intangible increases every day.

RADIATING
INTENT

IMAGE | A male warrior inscribes symbols onto a stone for the pyramid upon which the whole community is working. On his shoulder is perched a sacred bird, whose outstretched wing directs all this activity.

INTERPRETATION | This hexagram depicts the way purposefulness moves outward from the center, manifesting itself in ever-widening spheres of activity. The male warrior symbolizes the way of testing and training human nature that increases its versatility and fortitude. Inscribing symbols onto a stone means that you find your voice and perform acts of lasting meaning and value. That the stone fits into the pyramid means that your actions are part of a greater design of harmony, symmetry, and balance. The whole community working together on the same project symbolizes people united by a common vision. The sacred bird perched on the shoulder means that your spirit guide accompanies you everywhere and is always nearby. The wing directing all this activity symbolizes the guiding spirit's creative intent, which inspires both individuals and groups to devote their energy to something greater than themselves. Taken together, these symbols mean that far-reaching accomplishments can be achieved by conscientiously attuning yourself to your spirit guide's intent.

ACTION | The masculine half of the spirit warrior joins with others in order to advance as far as possible during a time of progress. The difficulty here is deciding which group to ally yourself with, as there are many competing for members. In a time when cooperation and collaboration produce great *benefit* for many, there still remain groups committed to authoritarianism and the control of resources. It is essential that you avoid groups serving only their own narrow interests and consider only those serving the widest possible good. In particular, avoid those repeating familiar catchwords and phrases in an attempt to hold their members to outworn ideologies and practices. You can recognize constructive and progressive groups by the startling aspects of their speech and action, which reflect your own emerging way of looking at the new and untried alternatives to failed solutions. Work with egalitarian groups whose wider vision is demonstrated by what they accomplish locally. Incorporate everyone into the work, include everyone who wishes to contribute: Together, you can make changes that bring *benefit* to others far beyond your sphere of activity. Above all, follow the spirit of intent: Do not hesitate to change groups if yours betrays its original and fundamental principles.

INTENT | Times of progress emerge from times of stagnation, times of advance follow times of hardship: A common vision emerges from shared adversity. When people no longer seek guidance from those with all the trappings of power and authority, then they create projects that are supported by their peers because they provide a meaningful outlet for people's pent-up energies. Because such projects are conceived from the ground up, they are the collective work of the community, made up of all the lives and talents and efforts and contributions of its members. It is a time when greatness is defined by community spirit, the totality of individual expressions bound together by a common purpose and shared lives. In an atmosphere of equality and creativity, people undertake altruistic projects voluntarily because they feel responsible to contribute to the whole of which they are a part.

SUMMARY | Your influence is growing, take care what you think. Act as though your every thought was being inscribed in stone. Live as though every moment is a stone upon which you are inscribing a wish. Dedicate each of these spirit-stones of your intent to the living pyramid of creation. Cultivate good will toward all. Collaborate with those of like mind. Help organize community endeavors.

THE LINE CHANGES

1ST   The instincts are part of the animal nature—they are powerful allies but they must follow and not lead. Study what motivates your body to do what it does—reflect on the direction this is taking you. Decide on the direction you want to go in and train your animal nature to help you get there.

2ND   This is a strong, well-balanced partnership—both of you are leaders but you work together rather than competing for recognition. Continue to go your own ways together—the destination you share benefits all. Your hard work will be rewarded—push forward.

3RD   The instinct to dominate others creates inferior superiors who make the lives of those under them miserable. Such people will always overstep their bounds. Give ground, pretend to be cowed, and the wrong-doer rushes into the trap—then appeal to a higher authority to enforce ethical standards.

4TH   The window of opportunity opens—both the inner and outer obstacles to success dissolve. All your experience gives both others and yourself confidence in your ability to take on a higher level of responsibility. Study the details of your duties—this proves key to re-establishing the balance.

5TH   When those who lead are good-hearted but without strong will, then people will lose focus, dissension will arise, and direction will drift aimlessly. You may hold on by not doing anything wrong, but this is not yet leadership. Move to a position more suited to your temperament.

6TH   Pushing ahead stubbornly brings you to a worrisome impasse. Stop here and look inside instead of outside—recognize that the real opponent is the one within and you can regain your momentum. Accept fault for going too far and work to make up for it—the conscience tames the animal nature.

DIGNIFYING
AMBITION

IMAGE | A male warrior climbs a great maze of thorns to behold a rose.

INTERPRETATION | This hexagram depicts the self-discipline required in order to follow our desires while neither suffering nor causing harm. The male warrior symbolizes the masculine creative force, who tests and trains human nature in order to increase its versatility and fortitude. The rose symbolizes longing and its power to transform abstractions into vital concrete goals. The thorns symbolize the dangers of greed, conceit, arrogance, incautiousness, possessiveness, self-righteousness, self-deceit, and self-indulgence. Taken together, these symbols mean that your vision of success leads you to strive only for goals that increase beauty, meaning, and well-being in the lives of others.

ACTION | The masculine half of the spirit warrior longs for the right things for the right reasons. Although longings have the power to motivate us to make extraordinary efforts to attain what eludes us, they can disrupt our lives if we have not refined our hearts and minds: The longing for fulfillment can make us strive for possessions and wealth; the longing for acknowledgment can make us strive for rank and reputation; the longing for correctness can make us deaf to criticism or new ideas; the longing for success can make us disregard warning signs and good advice; the longing for love can make us strive to possess or be possessed by others; the longing for the sacred can make us blind to its myriad manifestations; the longing for comfort can make us resist changing our perceptions of ourselves; the longing for freedom can make us slaves to our passions and senses. When we set aside self-interest, however, and genuinely strive for goals that bring *benefit* to others, then we ennoble even the most ambitious of endeavors and dignify even the most personal of longings. This is a time for making your desires worthy by ensuring that your motives are worthy. Because you will succeed in your endeavor, it is essential that you proceed free of blind ambition or ulterior motives. By training the mind to produce dignified thoughts and the heart to produce dignified feelings, you ensure the worthiness of your achievements.

INTENT | To desire something great and beautiful and powerful is to make ambition dignified, it is to dare to overcome any and all dangers, it is to reach the prize despite all personal hardships. The inevitability of your success, however, must not dull the cutting edge of your self-discipline. On the contrary, successfully bringing *benefit* to others carries the responsibility of ending matters as correctly as they were initiated. For this reason, it is essential that you maintain the quality of your self-discipline throughout the lifetime of your endeavor: Just as an endeavor that is begun incorrectly may be righted midway, an endeavor that is begun correctly may be ruined midway. Root out any and all undignified thoughts and feelings, making this a part of your spiritual practice that is performed every moment.

SUMMARY | Hardships and deprivations prove to serve a noble purpose. A breakthrough is close at hand, success is not far away. All your trials and suffering are not in vain. Keep your objective in view. Do not become distracted by wrongs done to you. Continue to focus on endeavors that strengthen and ennoble the human spirit. Do not become distracted by praise or recognition.

THE LINE CHANGES

1ST Taking advantage of others in any form causes them harm, even when your participation is indirect and unintentional. Set your will against any form of harming others since that will result in harm to yourself. Set aside self-interest and you will regain your momentum and direction.

2ND In chastising pets be strict, with strangers be lenient, and with those you know be unconditionally accepting. Being too harsh or impatient or overly critical creates an unintended backlash that will return to haunt you. Show through your actions and tone of voice what correctness looks like.

3RD Be aware of warning signs that signal a situation may be deteriorating to the point of becoming dangerous. Without overreacting, meet this situation head on—do not permit this to escalate further. Elicit advice from those more experienced as to the correct and balanced response.

4TH You must not allow your emotions to enter into this—it will be a long, drawn-out contest of wills and you will be baited often to act out of anger or outrage. Keep in mind that this is all about ethics and not personal. In public or private, exhibit the utmost ethical concern for the principles involved.

5TH Seeking justice, you find humanitarianism—acting on your own, you find allies. It was not your purpose when you began, but you have been defined by your battle. It was not your purpose when you began, but yours is a moral victory that will have repercussions long after you take your leave.

6TH Some elements of your personality go unquestioned, as if they were intrinsic and unalterable. This is wrong-headed—if you were taken at birth and raised in a faraway culture, your personality would be wholly different. Do not be stubborn—everyone else cannot be wrong and you right.

TRUSTING
INTUITION

IMAGE | Within her home, a female warrior listens closely to her dog barking excitedly at an approaching figure. Approaching her house from the wilderness, the shadowy figure of a man walks with a cane, bent over from the weight of what he carries on his back.

INTERPRETATION | The female warrior symbolizes the feminine creative force, who nurtures and encourages human nature in order to increase its sensitivity and loving-kindness. That she is in her home means that you rely on your inner resources and not others' opinions when deciding how to respond to change. The dog symbolizes the loyalty of the spirit companion, who helps guide us through life by alerting us to approaching changes that are not yet perceptible to our senses. That she listens attentively to the dog's barking means that you trust the spirit companion to alert you to change and do not ignore its warnings. That the approaching figure is shadowy and indistinct means that you wait until the impending change comes closer before deciding whether it is strange or familiar, threatening or promising. That he walks with a cane means that change comes slowly and that you have ample time to prepare for its arrival. The wilderness symbolizes the unexplored, unknown, and undomesticated realm. That he carries many things back from the wilderness means that you are open to the limitless possibilities change can bring. Just as the dog can tell her that the man approaches but cannot tell her what he carries, these symbols mean that although you trust intuition to tell you when change comes near, you do not expect it to tell you what kind of change is coming nor how you should respond to it.

ACTION | The feminine half of the spirit warrior relies on the intuition for help navigating the road of opportunity. Because the world is a web of intersecting strategies, rational thought and past experience cannot always be relied on to anticipate what lies just around the next bend of the road. Because others' strategies are based on misleading and confusing your rational thought, it is necessary to develop the insight to grasp the actual direction and momentum of change in a direct and intuitive way. Because others' strategies are based on taking advantage of the expectations you have derived from past experience, it is necessary to develop the insight to grasp the true potential of the future in a direct and intuitive way. Just as a ship creates a prow wake by pushing water ahead of itself, all strategies create prow wakes in the spirit realm. No matter how distant the strategy's origin or how much its effects may be attributed to random chance, its movement through the sea of spirit creates waves ahead of itself that the spirit companion senses and conveys as intuition. Listening closely to your spirit companion, you are able to avoid mistakes and seize opportunities, timing your decisions so that you neither move too soon nor too late.

INTENT | In training ourselves to trust the spirit companion, it is essential that we not mistake our own hopes and fears for genuine intuitions: The more we talk to ourselves, the more difficult it is for us to hear the spirit companion. Likewise, it is essential that we not be influenced by the hopes and fears of others: The more we listen to the insecurities of others, the more difficult it is for us to rely on our own inner sense of security. By constantly refining your relationship with the spirit companion, you become increasingly aware of the web of strategies making up the world. With the help of the spirit companion, you become attuned to the way in which spiritual intentions intersect one another, resulting in events that may be no further away from you than the lifespan of a mayfly or no nearer to you than the lifespan of a star. By reducing hopes and fears at this time, you find the whole world is your home and its changes are but the fields in which we sow and harvest.

SUMMARY | Your sensitivity is growing, take care what you believe. Calm the body's instinct for fearful watchfulness and hungry wakefulness. Calm the mind's habit of positive and negative imaginings. Calm the heart's reactions to the hopes and fears of others. Believe the song you still hear after all the static has been taken away. Seek a variety of opinions but act on your intuition.

THE LINE CHANGES

1ST Success comes very early to some, leading them to believe that they are somehow intrinsically superior to others. Such ingratitude and vanity are due to immaturity and cause long-term harm. Consider your legacy and the quality of the work you still wish to produce—keep learning.

2ND Some understand that success is beyond an individual's control, so they are humble and generous with their blessings. Donate your efforts to a worthwhile charity—or establish something reflecting your own values. Puncture the bubble around you and learn from those less fortunate than you.

3RD Some successful people do not believe they are bad judges of character, yet they listen only to self-serving flatterers while ignoring well-founded advice. Look for people you can learn from and do not trust those who gossip and slander. Do not cater to the superficial whims of the distracted.

4TH Some successful people hesitate to contradict the thinking of those above them—this is a lapse of ethics and causes long-term harm. Those above depend on you for solid information. Present what you know, its consequences, and viable responses in a way that challenges no one's authority.

5TH The window of opportunity opens—ultimate success depends on surrounding oneself with gifted people while adapting to circumstances without creating any resistance. Learn from all but depend on your intuition. You see the terrain ahead more clearly than those around you.

6TH Success comes late for some, leading them to believe they are less competitive and less materialistic than others—such ingratitude and vanity are due to envy and cause long-term harm. Every lifetime has its lessons to be learned. Your success and lessons are one and the same.

SYNCHRONIZING
MOVEMENT

IMAGE | Many different kinds of animals sing and dance and drum to the same rhythm. Above them shines the moon, which is shown as a water jar within which a rabbit crouches.

INTERPRETATION | This hexagram depicts the dance of renewal. The diverse group of animals means that you do not exclude any from your sphere of activity. Singing, dancing, and drumming to the same rhythm means that you work for the harmonious coordination of all involved. As a symbol of the womb and fertility, the moon overhead means that you attune yourself to the naturally repeating cycle of renewal that governs all things. Taken together, these symbols mean that in a time of transition, differences must be set aside in order to achieve the kind of coordinated effort it takes to succeed.

ACTION | As surely as the tides rise and fall, change overtakes us all. As things move toward one ending, they begin to shift toward another beginning. While everyone seems to be carried along by the same current of events, they do not all respond in the same way: Some compete, some cooperate, some withdraw, some lead. To thrive in such a climate, you need to form as broad an alliance as possible by joining forces with others regardless of past conflicts, distrust, or lack of familiarity. In this regard, past conflicts can be seen as the sparring by which you have trained each other in preparation for this greater test. Now is the time to prepare for the coming hardships that accompany periods of transition. Approach those who are resourceful and strong-willed, bridging differences by working toward goals that reflect your common interests. Increasingly integrate your efforts, concentrating on improving effectiveness, versatility, and mobility. Once it has a solid and proven foundation, open your alliance to others by accentuating the way in which the relationship would be mutually beneficial. It is essential to emphasize mutual respect among all concerned, demonstrating it by learning from new allies and integrating their methods into the overall strategy of the alliance as a whole. By continuing to expand your alliance in this way, you take part in a growing, organic response to events that succeeds because it does not lose its adaptability.

INTENT | The eternally recurring cycle of renewal moves at its own pace. It has its own rhythm and if we hope for our endeavors to succeed then we must time our actions in accord with the movement of the creative forces. Just as the tides fall into step with the phases of the moon, plants fall into step with the seasons, and dancers fall into step with the music, successful endeavors fall into step with the rising and falling energies of opportunity. Just as the seeds we plant next spring come from the harvest we store this winter, we will not position ourselves for the next period of advance if we enter this period of decline unprepared. Most people lack the agility to take advantage of opportunities during a period of new beginnings because they lacked the insight, discipline, and humility to keep time with the prior period of endings. Because you recognize that strong, flexible, mutually beneficial relationships are your greatest resource, however, you spend the winter setting the stage for next spring's sowing.

SUMMARY | You are attuned to the underlying harmony of the unseen forces. You have grown accustomed to the waxing and waning of the seasons and know how to recognize periods of advance and decline before they arrive. Without calling attention to yourself, try to help those around you succeed in good times and bad. By working for the success of others, you do not lose touch with the real.

THE LINE CHANGES

1ST   Take up the new form of self-discipline you have been consider-
      ing, incorporating it into your regimen. Increasing your strength,
      flexibility, and endurance will make you feel better prepared for
      the challenge ahead. Link your physical training to your spiritual
      practice.

2ND   The window of opportunity opens—you can change things for
      the better now. Having gained the trust and confidence of a supe-
      rior, do not betray it by overstepping your bounds or failing to
      fulfill your responsibilities. Keep your focus on the plan and
      avoid personality conflicts.

3RD   When mean-spirited people are set in charge, they value money
      over ethics. This bodes ill because it means they have the sup-
      port of those above. If you remain loyal to such people you will
      share their fate—approach others outside the situation who may
      be able to exert pressure for the better.

4TH   When your opponent adapts to your strategy and counters with
      a brilliant move, do not blunder ahead with your plan. Recognize
      when you have been outflanked and withdraw before you suffer
      real loss. Pretend greater weakness than you have, buying time
      to prepare your next move.

5TH   When a former ally betrays your trust and breaks the conditions
      of a long-standing agreement, you have no choice but to fulfill
      your duties and protect those in your charge. Someone experi-
      enced and ready to retire will make the best leader. Don't give
      young ambitious people the lead position.

6TH   You prevail after much strife and bad blood—the bitterness will
      stand in the way of reconciliation for a long time to come. Do not
      let your guard down now—every effort will be made to under-
      mine the terms of the new treaty. The victors want to forget it
      all quickly, the losers can never forget.

SUSTAINING
RESILIENCE

IMAGE | A female warrior stands by the sea, facing a strong, unceasing wind. She stands naked, with her arms outstretched, allowing the wind to coil around her without resistance. Along the shore, the remains of others who have stood in that same wind are depicted as old tree stumps devoid of life.

INTERPRETATION | This hexagram represents the inner flexibility needed to withstand external change. The sea symbolizes the vast, unknown possibilities before you. The female warrior symbolizes the way of nurturing and encouraging human nature that increases its sensitivity and loving-kindness. That she faces the wind of ever-shifting changes means that you preserve what is essential by adopting an attitude of unrelenting fluidity. That she is naked means that you are unafraid to stand exposed to the elements of change. That she stands with open arms means that you withstand change by accepting the situation and patiently waiting for it to pass. The dead trees symbolize those who attempt to resist change in the wrong way, relying on mere stubbornness and inflexibility where continued growth and adaptability are called for. Taken together, these symbols mean that inner flexibility and adaptability can be sustained forever by allowing change to pass through you like the open sky allows the wind to pass through it.

ACTION | The feminine half of the spirit warrior undergoes countless transformations in order to remain whole. When we respond to difficulties and hardship by clinging to our past conceptions of ourselves, we become rigid and resentful, eventually losing the very sense of self we sought to protect and becoming exactly the kind of person we least sought to emulate. This is a time for keeping your focus on bringing *benefit* to others: Just as a cloud's appearance is constantly changed by the wind until it has poured its rain out upon the thirsty land, this is a time for letting go of past self-concepts in order to be transformed by life into a better servant of life. While many set out on this path, few follow it to the end. To sustain a sincere attitude of resilience year after year, it is necessary to devote yourself to something greater than yourself—to something that gives your sacrifices meaning and worth. Do not become dispirited because your ideals and vision are not widely accepted by those around you—instead, look at the lives such people are leading and ask yourself if you wish to follow in their footsteps. By increasingly taking on the nature of the wind itself, you become an ever more positive force of transformation in the world.

INTENT | In the midst of so much change, it is important not to isolate or alienate yourself from others. It is a time for establishing new alliances as well as for maintaining existing relationships wherever practicable. It is not just that you benefit from the support and camaraderie of others at this time, but that your presence also adds significantly to their lives. In situations where the end of a relationship is part and parcel of the difficulties you face, it is essential that you not withdraw into yourself and try to withstand the turbulence by stubbornly clinging to a vision of the past. Mimic the rain cloud, allow yourself to be changed by the wind of change, and find the kind of relationships where your contributions are accepted as nourishment. By holding fast to your allies, you are able to recover from hardships easily and use those experiences to bring others *benefit*. By adapting to all manner of circumstances without losing your intrinsic self, you retain the suppleness of youth even as you gain the wisdom of the elder spirits.

SUMMARY | Though you are buffeted by change, you continue to grow because you do not hold rigidly to your vision of the past. Though deprived of the stability and security you would like, you continue to thrive because you do not hold rigidly to your vision of the future. In the midst of the storm, you continue to advance because you join forces with the wind. Time is your ally, change is your ally.

The Line Changes

1ST   Looking at matters from different perspectives is beneficial unless it paralyzes you—if you wait for the perfect plan, you will never make a decision. Trust in your ability to adjust to changing circumstances. Calculated risks lead to incalculable rewards.

2ND   People who overwhelm you with too much intimacy too soon are a pastime at best and a danger at worst. It is painful learning that not everyone has the generosity of spirit you have. Look for someone who has learned the same lesson—then allow matters to evolve slowly.

3RD   To seek intimacy out of loneliness or insecurity leads to heartache and regret. The force of your personality may overwhelm your peers for now, but their growing dependence on you will soon ensnare you. You have not yet correctly adapted to your surroundings.

4TH   You are able to establish strong partnerships in every aspect of your life. Others are as interested in you as you are in them—mutual regard leads to mutual benefit. You have successfully adapted to your surroundings—do not stop trying to benefit the people and nature around you.

5TH   You achieve a position of responsibility and grow comfortable making important decisions. But do not grow overconfident or complacent—consider the consequences of your decisions both before and after making them. The higher you climb the ladder, the more visible you make yourself.

6TH   To try to benefit all does not mean trying to please everyone—it means envisioning the greater good and contributing to that with each thought, word, and action. Be responsible for your contribution and you succeed. Be responsible for others' contributions and you fail.

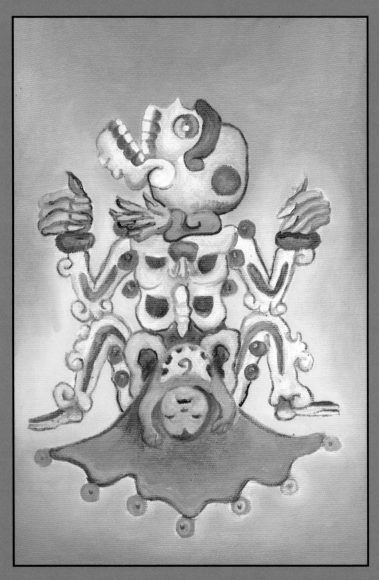

TRANSFORMING
EXTINCTION

IMAGE | The skeletal form of death is shown in the childbirth position, giving birth to new life. Both the blood accompanying the birth and the bones of the skeleton have jade beads affixed to them. Over the heart of the newborn is the spiral cross-section of a conch shell.

INTERPRETATION | This hexagram represents the immortality that is born from mortality. The skeletal form of death symbolizes those remains of an individual that are common to all people. The newborn symbolizes the spirit warrior, who is delivered from the body's death to return to the spirit realm from whence it comes. The jade beads affixed to the blood symbolize the precious nature of that which sustains life. The jade beads affixed to the bones of the skeleton symbolize the precious nature of all those who have come before us. The spiral of the conch over the heart symbolizes the wisdom and power of divine intelligence that fills the soul of the newborn spirit warrior. Taken together, these symbols mean that your body is the womb within which the embryo of the spirit warrior is carried.

ACTION | The spirit warrior contemplates the inevitable extinction of the body's spark in order to illuminate the perfection of the present moment. It is a time for studying the end of things, for opening the heart fully to the reality of death. The need here is to reach beyond the intellect's dead rationality in order to grasp the emotional reality of the body's mortality. Instead of waiting for death to approach you, take the lead and approach it in order to experience that part of yourself that does not die. Because you have the courage to authentically accept the end of bodily experience, your heart fills with joyous appreciation for each moment that blossoms anew with the timeless perfection of creation. Because you have the loving-kindness to authentically accept that death inspires fear and doubt in other people, you find ways to express your emotions that encourage others to gaze unflinchingly into the bittersweet awareness of mortal perfection. Those who continue to avert their eyes from death's face, see imperfection everywhere and find it uncomfortable to genuinely contemplate or discuss their mortality. Those who treat death as the midwife who delivers them into the ancestral homeland of the spirit warriors, however, increasingly come to view creation through the eyes of the immortal that is being born every moment. Because you prepare for the end of things, you are ready for the beginning that lies beyond.

INTENT | Knowing that death transforms us after the body's light is extinguished requires little more than intellectual knowledge. Knowing that we transform death before the body's light is extinguished, however, requires firsthand experience of the deathless. For the spirit warrior, death is not the absence of life. It is the felt presence of the gateway between the visible and invisible realms—it is the loving presence of the guide home. We transform the extinction of the body by becoming the spirit warrior who carries its spark back to the universal fire of creation. We transform the way we view the world by appreciating the preciousness of every moment we are honored to spend in the visible realm.

SUMMARY | Your spirit is growing stronger, take care what you create. Keep in mind the end of things and you will begin only what you wish to be remembered for—keep in mind the unpredictability of fate and you will not waste time or energy or petty goals. Transform death into your ally and you will make every moment count. Transform death into the spirit of renewal and you will find peace of mind.

THE LINE CHANGES

1ST   When those around you are swayed by fads and fashions, correct your own inclination to follow along. When others around you are swayed by the unrelenting torrent of events, do not go along with their emotions. Make a center where external events do not change your state of mind.

2ND   You can stabilize yourself but not another—each person must come to it in their own time and with their own effort. Even when you are dragged forward by impetuous allies, do not allow their disturbed emotions to become your own. Offer advice—but if it is ignored, remain unmoved by the backlash.

3RD   Those below don't follow you because you don't trust their advice—those above don't give you full rein because they don't trust your judgment. You are in a no-win situation and growing more frustrated with every episode. You should cultivate patience and self-evaluation or else step down.

4TH   Those above trust you because you avoid complicating simple things—those below respect you because you do not make snap judgments. This is a position of responsibility but you are capable of much more. Continue to excel here and you will be rewarded with advancement.

5TH   It is difficult to see at first that your words are really actions, as concrete as an attack or a retreat. Once you see the force of words in this realm, however, you adapt quickly and correctly. Proper speech not only demonstrates your own inner stability, but helps others feel less uncertain.

6TH   The window of opportunity opens—you are able to achieve the ecstatic life. Neither the uncertainties of life or the certainty of death throws you off balance—you are becoming a mountain of immovable wisdom. Hold still—all of creation is passing your way.

EMBRACING
NONINTERFERENCE

IMAGE | Many different kinds of animals gather peacefully to drink from the river of life.

INTERPRETATION | This hexagram depicts the single source of life, from which every life receives its rightful share. The different kinds of animals symbolize the various needs, wants, and interests of those involved. The river of life symbolizes the resources to sustain all. That the animals gather peacefully to drink from the river means that all concerned have enough and do not need to compete with one another to ensure their well-being. Taken together, these symbols mean that you help create a time of peace and prosperity for all concerned.

ACTION | Just as the river is a material blessing bringing water to everything equally, the feminine creative force is an invisible presence bringing *benefit* to all equally. It is a time for trusting that *need* is being met even if you cannot see how. In practice, this means that it is essential that people and events be allowed to develop naturally, without any outside interference. In this sense, it is important that you resist interfering with others as diligently as you resist the efforts of others to interfere with you. It is a delicate time and one that is easily misinterpreted. It does not call for isolationism or callous disregard of others' suffering but, rather, for impartial benevolence. Nature does not show its impartiality by ceasing to provide air, water, and food to all. Nor does it show its benevolence by giving air, water, and food to some and not to others. Because you mimic nature you give to each all that you can according to the season—and you do so without using your gifts as leverage by which to influence the actions of others. Likewise, you are most careful when accepting gifts or assistance at this time: Sensing there are conditions placed on your acceptance, you look elsewhere for assistance because accepting the wrong type of favor in this climate is particularly ill-timed. In all your interactions with others, be on guard against your own ulterior motives as vigilantly as you guard against the ulterior motives of others. Because you are attuned to the positive value of impartial benevolence, you become a well of *benefit* nurturing the right of others to make their own decisions and determine their own destiny.

INTENT | When people interfere in the rightful destiny of others, they create a backlash of resentment and retribution that inevitably surfaces to strike them back. For this reason, self-interest is best served by not intervening in the decisions or development of others. When relationships reflect the mutual respect of warriors who are able to exercise self-control, then alliances thrive, creating harmony, contentment, and well-being for all their members. When we bring *benefit* as impartially as the river waters all it touches, then we are welcomed into the invisible presence of the feminine creative force as lovingly as we have embraced all we have touched.

SUMMARY | Things are going as they should. Refrain from trying to change them at this time. Let matters take their natural course. Intervening now will create greater problems for all concerned. Demonstrating trust and respect now will create greater opportunities for all concerned. Where you are unsure, investigate matters more deeply, seeking greater understanding rather than initiating action.

THE LINE CHANGES

1ST Standing out from the crowd is no cause for celebration—this draws unwanted attention and impinges on your freedom to act. Do not display your talents or understanding now—focus on independence, not recognition. Do not associate with those who are reckless or ambitious.

2ND When a relationship enters a phase of emotional darkness, it often seems easier to end it than to repair it. But that decision is often made out of grief for the ideal that has been lost. If you show you are committed to seeing this through at all costs, the other may be reassured enough to try.

3RD A small band of dedicated allies can bring down a much stronger regime—but victory is never as swift or complete as one imagines. The greater the success, the more time must pass before its effects take hold. Know when you have won and let others supervise the long-term reorganization.

4TH When you have served inside an organization for a while, you know its real intentions. When you know those to be corrupted, leave and join another organization where your firsthand knowledge can be put to good use. In time, you may return to help your former peers redeem themselves.

5TH Ethical behavior does not mean always telling the truth, for to tell a tyrant the truth may result in the harming of an innocent. Deceiving the corrupted in order to benefit the innocent is high ethical behavior. Your light must be veiled during this conflict, but it will shine brilliantly afterward.

6TH Strength is not more powerful than wisdom, ruthlessness is not more effective than ethics. The high and mighty may have their day but their fall will be remembered for years. The pendulum is about to swing out of darkness again—be patient a while longer and plan for what follows.

CONTROLLING
CONFRONTATION

IMAGE | A male warrior stands silhouetted against the setting sun, his shadow cast upon the ground before him. He is armed with spear and shield and is in the prime of life. He stands alone in the world, apart from companions or dwellings.

INTERPRETATION | This hexagram depicts the single source of light from which every body receives its shadow. The male warrior symbolizes the masculine creative force, who tests and trains human nature in order to increase its versatility and fortitude. The inert and inanimate shadow symbolizes the enemy-within, the self-defeating part of every human being. The setting sun symbolizes the ending of a phase of strength and influence. The spear and shield symbolize the skills of attack and defense. The prime of life symbolizes the work that must be accomplished while the creative force still waxes. Standing alone in the wilderness symbolizes the work of self-transformation, which cannot be perfected through the efforts or experiences of others. Taken together, these symbols mean that you succeed by mastering destructive passions.

ACTION | The masculine half of the spirit warrior accumulates force in order to resist the use of force. Whether they are internal or external, it is necessary to confront the forces working in opposition to our goals. This is a matter of grave delicacy, however, since the passions tied to self-interest run equally deep and strong among all concerned. Old grievances and resentments, in particular, stand in the way of a peaceful and mutually advantageous resolution to the current discord. For this reason, confronting others means we are forced to confront ourselves, restraining our own anger and righteous indignation by seeing how our own actions have contributed to the present conflict. Only by holding our anger in check can we avoid escalating the problem at hand: An uncompromising stance of having been wronged serves no one's purposes here since it merely forces others to do the same. The danger is that real hostility can be ignited under these conditions—hostility that can inflict profound suffering on all concerned and take a long time for any party to heal. This is a time to treat your opposition with all the respect due a great warrior: Avoid inflammatory and provocative statements based on half-truths or a one-sided view of things, since slyly provoking others to hostility is doubly hostile. This is likewise a time to act like a great warrior: Accept responsibility for past mistakes and make good faith commitments to remedy injustices and imbalances among all concerned immediately, since demanding that others right their wrongs without following suit is doubly wrong. For the spirit warrior, true force is exercised by not resorting to hostility even when it promises the shortest route to success.

INTENT | Those who are secure in their ability to survive and adapt find no fear or insecurity in their shadow. Those who are secure in their ability to love and be loved find no mean-spiritedness or hate in their shadow. Those who are secure in their ability to imbue their shadow with light find no self-defeating actions in their shadow. For this reason, fears and insecurities are calls for us to strengthen some weakness or vulnerability, just as mean-spiritedness and hate are calls for us to break the chains of alienation binding us. By taking up the work of self-transformation, we purify the shadow and make it radiant. When there is nothing left by which we can defeat ourselves, we have answered the shadow's call to make ourselves impervious to any defeat from the outside.

SUMMARY | There is much to lose by forcing others to confront what they are not prepared for. It is in your best interests to de-escalate confrontation and move matters along more slowly. Because former allies make the worst enemies, take the time to disengage in a manner that attracts the least hostility. Be willing to let the opposition win a last battle so that you might win the war. Control yourself so that others may feel secure enough to do the same.

THE LINE CHANGES

1ST Avoid extremes in any facet of your lifestyle—distance yourself from those whose tastes are immoderate or behavior is suspicious. Keep in mind that people who flaunt their improprieties are not steadfast allies when their backs are to the wall. If you wish to be taken seriously, live seriously.

2ND Those accustomed to conflict no longer feel themselves bleeding, those who come to enjoy the bickering of power struggles no longer see others bleeding. Here compromise must take the form of action—give in. Do anything to break the deadlock before it is too late—make the first move.

3RD Competing with peers brings nothing but misfortune. There is no gain to be had by allowing those above to pit you against others in the same straits. Comport yourself with dignity and integrity at all times—do not compromise your values or self-respect.

4TH Recognize when you have made an error in judgment and admit it readily. You are like a fish out of water here, so there is real advantage to asking for direction from any around you. They will remember your humility even after you get your footing and your worth becomes apparent.

5TH The window of opportunity opens—there is a perfect resolution possible. Both sides are exaggerating—ignore their claims and counterclaims and determine what each most fears losing. Protect the real interests of each and they will follow your lead in resolving the smaller matters.

6TH Victory is an illusion—it creates a backlash that returns to harm you and yours. Righteous indignation is a trap—it creates resentment for years to come. Let desire, ambition, and emotion run away with you and you will have cause to regret it for a long, long time.

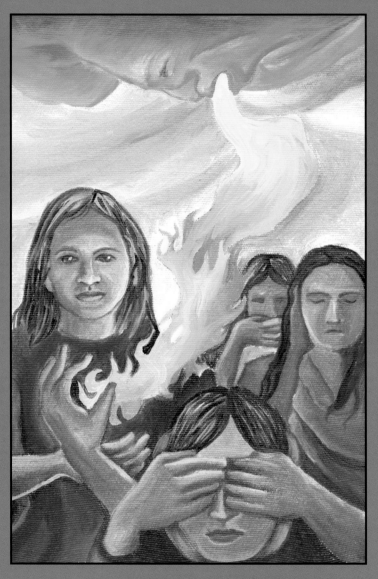

ACCEPTING
INSTRUCTION

IMAGE | Fire descends from the sky of the creators, entering the only receptive heart it finds among a group of female warriors.

INTERPRETATION | This hexagram depicts truth and its power to overcome the fear of rejection and aloneness. The fire descending from the sky of the creators symbolizes the transmission of divine intelligence passing from the sky-realm of the ancestors into the earth-realm of the living. The three warriors oblivious to the divine fire represent social conventions and their power to maintain the status quo. The single female warrior who opens her heart to the divine fire represents the individual who places greater trust in the teachings of spirit than in the accepted wisdom of the time. Taken together, these symbols mean that you do not hesitate to walk the road of freedom alone.

ACTION | The feminine half of the spirit warrior gains understanding of a truth that can neither be seen, heard, or spoken. While much useful knowledge can be learned from others, the core lesson of life can only be experienced firsthand through our relationship with the divine. Until this central lesson of life is learned, all other knowledge revolves around the central concept of our physical and social identity. Just as we invent simple explanations to make adult reasoning understandable to children, the concept of a physical and social self is a temporary explanation to make the spirit warrior's reasoning understandable to us until we experience the divine. Because you are leaving intermediaries behind in your spirit journey, it is a time for ridding yourself of misunderstandings and misconceptions learned in an earlier phase of life. The greater part of learning is relearning. Because many of the ideas you harbor are the result of earlier naiveté and inexperience, they must be replaced with ideas that more accurately portray the world as it truly is. Making your heart open by allowing yourself to be loved, receiving divine intelligence by accepting instruction from your spiritual ancestors, you become a torch that helps dispel the shadows of doubt and fear clouding the hearts of others.

INTENT | When you have experienced a lesson that cannot be communicated to others, hold it in your heart, protect it and nourish it, concerning yourself only with the question of how and under what circumstances to put it into action. By holding it in your heart you do not waste energy trying to explain the inexplicable nor run the risk of calling undue attention to yourself. By protecting it you concentrate on your knowledge in order to keep the flame of understanding alive. By nourishing it you continue to learn its deeper meanings in order to help the flame of understanding grow. By concerning yourself only with putting it into practice in the right way at the right time, you bring *benefit* to others while honoring the spiritual path they have chosen. For the spirit warrior, all other knowledge revolves around the core lesson of experiencing the divine.

SUMMARY | Only the wise are truly humble, only the humble are truly open-hearted. Make every action ring with humility and sincerity. Focus on the immediacy of your senses—what you are seeing, hearing, smelling, tasting, and touching in the moment—and not on what you are thinking, feeling, and remembering. Let go of the self-importance of the inside, let spirit enter your heart from the outside. Pay close attention to the details of your surroundings.

THE LINE CHANGES

1ST   In the course of trying to salvage something slipping away, you unexpectedly meet a superior who treats you like an equal. Follow the advice you are given and your inner riches will exceed your outer riches. It's a uniquely positive partnership—sustain it through your coming transformations.

2ND   You stand before your overflowing treasure house and think yourself poor because the jewel you loved most was flawed. But possession is not love and a person cannot be won or lost—return to what is present, not absent, in your life. Your kindness and sincerity will lead you to happiness.

3RD   When the impasse is on the inside, no direction outside leads anywhere—all undertakings come to a halt and darkness obscures hope. Nothing changes until you change your habits of thought and emotion. Do not stay here grieving for what does not exist—follow those who know this terrain.

4TH   You do not know why this one comes to you and that one does not—but you must serve each that approaches as an equal. Unseen forces pull you together so that you might help release the other's untapped potential. The benefit you dispense now comes back to you a hundredfold later.

5TH   You can extend your good fortune by viewing your accomplishments as the foundation of a higher and more noble endeavor. Fit the most far-sighted and capable people together like pieces of a puzzle, the whole of which exceeds the sum of its individuals. Aspire to meaningful beauty.

6TH   Once a wave crests, it is inevitable that it falls—once creative momentum is expended, it is time to stop. But this does not mean withdrawing into yourself. Be accessible and return to where you started by nurturing others' potential.

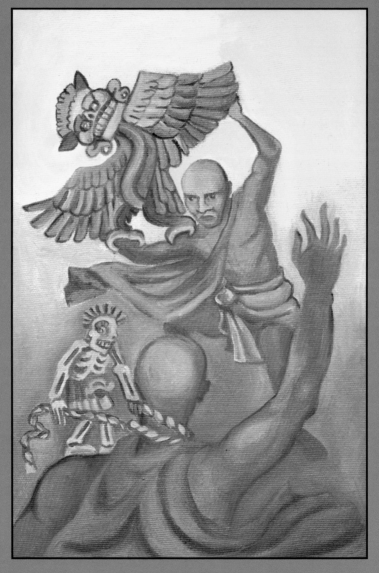

EVOKING
OPPOSITE

IMAGE | Two male warriors engage in conflict. One holds an owl on his arm, waving it at his opponent. The other has a small figure of death on his shoulder that is strangling him with a rope.

INTERPRETATION | This hexagram depicts the way opposites may be used to bring about peace, harmony, and contentment. The conflict between male warriors represents the struggle of people or ideas to dominate one another. The owl symbolizes the opponent's weaknesses—in this case, the fear of death. Waving the owl at an opponent symbolizes the use of others' weaknesses in order to unnerve them and break their will for battle. The figure of death strangling the opponent symbolizes others' self-defeating habits of thought and action that prevent them from successfully overcoming us. Taken together, these symbols mean that you succeed because you make your opponent's weaknesses your ally.

ACTION | The masculine half of the spirit warrior resorts to spiritual protection in order to avoid direct confrontation or hostility. When efforts to make peace fail and adversarial relationships cannot be healed and our adversaries take it upon themselves to escalate tensions through intimidation, then we find that our intentions for peace and self-restraint and nonintervention harbor equally powerful intentions in the form of their opposites. In order to mobilize these other facets of your intention, however, it is necessary to first look inside and see how your own fears and weaknesses are being used against you. By seeing how debilitating and demoralizing it is to be attacked from within, you can begin to aim your spiritual intent at the fears and weaknesses of your opponent. Because each of us has this enemy-within who attacks us with our own fears and insecurities, it is not difficult to conceive of your opponent's own enemy-within. Rather than trying to visualize any specific traits or fears or weaknesses, simply allow yourself to feel the presence of your own enemy-within and, knowing that your opponent's is intrinsically the same, aim your intent to make an ally of your opponent's enemy-within, offering it support and help and nurture. By strengthening the enemy-within of others, you allow them to defeat themselves from within: Haunted by strange dreams and intrusive fears and unnerving memories and unending ruminations, your opponent increasingly loses the self-confidence and passion to pursue an external conflict. Because you evoke the enemy-within of others only as a last resort, you are able to share a life of peace, harmony, and contentment with those around you.

INTENT | Even our enemy-within has an enemy-within. By turning the strategy of spiritual protection inward and aiming your intention at the enemy-within of your own fears and weaknesses, you nurture the opposite within your opposite: Ally yourself with the self-defeating part within your self-defeating part and you deprive your enemy-within of its power to rob you of your creative energy and meaningful accomplishments. Undermine your own enemy-within by acknowledging your positive intentions and constructive actions. When we keep in mind that a large part of our self-defeating behavior comes from apathy, rationalization, and emotional detachment, we can see that some of the most prominent features of the enemy-within are ingrained excuses for inaction. For this reason, it is essential that we be able to summon the will to direct action when necessary: The line of least resistance sometimes passes through unavoidable resistance and requires that we act in a manner directly opposite to our personal preferences. For the spirit warrior, there is no greater victory than defeating the enemy-within.

SUMMARY | Know your opponents better than they know themselves. Understand their weak points and know how to exploit them. Defeat your opponent's will to fight and you avoid much needless suffering. Because this conflict is not of your making, move steadily and confidently to show that you are ready to bring your opponent's worst fears out into the open. Act without anger or ambition.

THE LINE CHANGES

1ST Because of all the conditioning people are exposed to from birth on, nothing is more difficult to attain than naturalness. You have the good fortune to know the social and familial influences on you and to be dedicated to mitigating them. You are a seasoned wayfarer on the road of freedom.

2ND Very few people do things with no purpose in mind, yet acting without any expectation is the only way to create a wide-open arena in which anything at all might happen. Trust the world enough that you can play with it. Think in terms of mystery and discovery, not gain and loss.

3RD Because you follow your own rules and not the rule of self-interest, you alone are trusted by those above. Because they follow the rule of gain and loss, your peers cannot be trusted to reorganize things for the next phase. Do not become cautious now—complete your task, then move on.

4TH Because you do not follow the rule of self-interest, your motives are a mystery—this means you cannot be controlled, or trusted, by those above. Being excluded from such an oppressive group, however, frees you up to remain creative. They have better resources, you have better choices.

5TH Being unswervingly loyal to your principles does not mean letting people pigeonhole you. Don't fall into the trap of speaking and acting as others expect you to. If water stops flowing, it becomes stagnant—if you stop responding spontaneously, you become what you have stood against.

6TH The time for creative expansion is over—you must move into the next phase with meticulous planning and tactful reserve. Failing to adapt your temperament to these more complicated times will result in real setbacks. Pay attention to how others are changing and mirror them.

HOLDING
BACK

IMAGE | A mother bird protects her eggs from a young fox by pretending to be wounded. The blue speech glyphs show that she calls attention to herself in order to lead the fox away from her nest. The fox is distracted by what he perceives as easy prey, ready to be led further and further away from the defenseless eggs.

INTERPRETATION | This hexagram depicts the strategy of confusion and misdirection. The bird symbolizes the one who is seeking to protect something vulnerable and valuable. The fox symbolizes the one who is seeking to take something vulnerable and valuable. The eggs symbolize the goals, accomplishments, and needs of both. The mother bird calling attention to herself by feigning injury represents the tactic of appealing to the greed, ambition, and laziness of an opponent. The young fox getting distracted and led away from his goal by the allure of easy pickings represents the short-sightedness and excitability of the inexperienced. Taken together, these symbols mean that you study the motives of others so that you can mislead them—and see through their attempts to mislead you—as circumstances require.

ACTION | The spirit warrior is sometimes the nesting bird and sometimes the hunting fox: Whenever the opportunity for loss and gain presents itself, each side attempts to mislead the other without being misled themselves. Those attempting to prevent a long-range loss try to hide what they most value and offer up a kind of sacrifice they believe their opponent will mistake for the genuine prize. Pretending to be flushed from cover early and acting the part of a flustered and clumsy strategist, such warriors must gamble by offering up something truly valuable if they are to make the bait irresistible enough to distract the opponent from the real prize. For this reason, the bait is not successful if it just misdirects another's attention—it must also stall matters by tiring the pursuer, making what looked simple and easily acquired increasingly complex and less attainable. Likewise, those attempting to acquire a long-range gain try to ignore short-term distractions and remain focused on uncovering the real prize. Impatience and overconfidence are the surest signs of inexperience in such warriors. Pausing to consider why an opponent might surrender too much too soon, the experienced warrior ignores distractions and continues to follow the original scent.

INTENT | Whether you are the pursuer or the pursued, this is a time for holding back: Where the mother bird tries to hold back the hunting fox from discovering her nest, the hunting fox tries to hold back his first reaction to jump at every opportunity. In the world of nature, both the nesting bird and the hunting fox are spirit warriors. Every moment of every day is a battle for survival of the individual and the bloodline. Each moment of each day requires unbroken attention to the strategies that enable them to successfully play their part in the ongoing work of creation. True spirit warriors master the art of holding back by studying what motivates others—and themselves—to act as they do. The nesting bird succeeds because she knows the fox chases anything that runs from it; the hunting fox succeeds because he knows the bird runs away from the nest to protect her eggs. Study what others hold valuable, study what you yourself hold valuable, and you can successfully act on the purposes you perceive behind every action.

SUMMARY | Slow things down and analyze them rationally. Don't act on your first reaction. Consider the deeper motives others might have for their actions. Consider how others might likewise be considering your deeper motives. Wait for them to make another move. Create a maze of options for your opponent to negotiate. Use delays and distractions to wear the other side down.

THE LINE CHANGES

1ST   Someone you care about needs financial assistance and you cannot help as much as you wish. Even the help you can give is a real sacrifice if the loan is not repaid. Help as much as possible without it actually creating hardship—once loaned, however, put the matter out of your mind.

2ND   Those close to you need more of your attention and affection. At first this seems an unreasonable request, since you are already overburdened, but later you see the need motivating it. Don't reject them—exercise unconditional acceptance and find a way to include them in your other activities.

3RD   If you try collaborating with your peers, their petty goals drive you out of the group. If you try working along similar lines on your own, their petty insecurities pull you into the group. If they will not raise their goals, go on without them—do not allow them to trivialize your contribution.

4TH   Having achieved your goal, you reach a plateau, unsure of what course to take next. In this sense, success feels like a let-down and a kind of stagnation sets in. Cast about for someone who is like you were at the beginning—including this person in your plans will reinvigorate you.

5TH   The window of opportunity opens—your kind-heartedness and the purity of your intention allow others to contribute gratefully to your efforts. Continue to evince the highest ethical standards—do not risk even the appearance of impropriety. Target all your gifts to benefit those you serve.

6TH   Your needs diminish while you have more and more. You find assistance everywhere you go since you no longer need a fixed dwelling place to know who you are or why you are here. Simply embody a wellspring of *benefit* that overflows into the lives of all you meet—live the ecstatic life.

STABILIZING
COMMUNION

IMAGE | In the light of the full moon there blooms a wondrous flower, whose petals grow in the form of speech glyphs. In an otherwise empty and desolate wilderness, a female warrior shares the flower with a gigantic butterfly.

INTERPRETATION | This hexagram depicts the attunement of spirit to spirit. The full moon symbolizes the height of the female warrior's power. The flower symbolizes the fleeting perfection of every blossoming moment. The petals that grow in the form of speech glyphs show that it is the flower's essence that calls kindred spirits together. The wilderness symbolizes a place that appears on the surface to be lonely and deserted. The female warrior means that you nurture, and are nurtured by, everything that touches you. The butterfly means that you are accompanied by the spirit of a great warrior who has returned from the house of the sun to inspire and encourage the living. Taken together, these symbols mean that you achieve a lasting intimacy with nature, other people, and the divine.

ACTION | The feminine half of the spirit warrior sets the past and future aside in order to be absorbed in the present. We separate ourselves from the world around us when we focus on our own emotions and listen to our own thoughts. While there are times for introspection, constantly ruminating on internal experiences stunts our development at the stage of the physical and social identity. In order to develop the spiritual identity, it is necessary to train awareness to move past its preoccupation with the strictly personal and to sense itself immersed in the sea of spirit encompassing all creation. Introspection loses its effectiveness when it merely reinforces existing problems by going over them time and time again. Problems that cannot be solved by introspection can be dissolved by experiencing the commingling of spiritual identities. This is a time to achieve spiritual equilibrium, eliminating the fluctuations of mood and the habits of thought by sensing the unitary nature of all creation. For this reason, communion seems like a different kind of sense perception, one that allows us to sense the single body of spirit beyond our body's senses. By attuning your awareness to the single awareness unifying the whole, you stabilize your emotions and thoughts in the present moment, taking away their power to interrupt your spiritual rapport with nature, other people, and the divine. By making communion with the greater world beyond you your priority, you enjoy a prolonged period of contentment and success.

INTENT | The barriers between you and the world dissolve the more you revere the sacred nature of all existence: Sensing the universal essence common to everything whose existence you share, you move permanently beyond fear and insecurity into wonder and joy. While developing the sense of communion is intoxicating and rewarding, it remains the first step in an unfinished journey until the time that your habits of emotion and thinking are stabilized. When you sense the world as a sea binding all its drops into a single present, no longer interrupted by images of the past and future, you solidify your spiritual identity and feel yourself at one with all things. Intimate with nature, people, and the divine, you transform yourself endlessly without ever changing. Everywhere you go, you meet your twin.

SUMMARY | You enter a period of tranquility and peace of mind, one in which goals and obstacles are set aside in favor of sharing moments of purposeless activity with who and what you love. Set aside the need to be productive by immersing yourself in an extended time-out: Focus on profoundly appreciating spirit radiating from every blissful form and you merge, like a tear of bliss, into the sea of bliss.

THE LINE CHANGES

1ST   You recognize that others are responding to something you cannot quite make out—like an itch you can't scratch, it demands more attention. This is the barely perceptible influence ever circulating between people. Like any of your other senses, the more finely it is tuned, the more it perceives.

2ND   You recognize another, immediately certain they play an important role in your life. Yet this person does not respond immediately—though accessible, they proceed cautiously, like one not trusting their instincts. Slow down, match the other's pace—this is most favorable in the long run.

3RD   Your patience and character are sorely tested—the one you belong with is inaccessible and the one you should avoid is willing. Don't focus on aloneness—focus on the kind of conduct that will convince the right one. Not being serious here will only ensure your aloneness.

4TH   The window of opportunity opens—the influence you feel between you and your companions is felt by them, too. This heartfelt bond allows you all to move as one. You will achieve your goal but it will not be as fulfilling as expected.

5TH   You have a responsibility to those above as well as those below—and much of your success comes from being sensitive to the needs of both. Neither of them cares about the other's needs and both are demanding your support. Ignore pressure and hold to the highest ethical standard.

6TH   People are defined by what they are sensitive to—the influence circulating between people is not always of the best intent. When others flatter you and tell you secrets in confidence, they seek to sway you without your consent. You should sense this as they approach and shut them out.

PENETRATING
CONFUSION

IMAGE | Two hands try to make their way through a tangle of vines.

INTERPRETATION | The two hands symbolize our power to grasp events, sort them by feel, and fashion them into meaningful experiences. The tangle of vines symbolizes the complications that arise when we allow ourselves to become overly involved in situations that lie off our true path. Taken together, these symbols mean that you rely on your innate strengths to get free of confusion and regain your momentum.

ACTION | It is a time for seeing through entanglements. Confusion arises when our vision is blurred by false reasoning or past emotions. Seeing through confusion requires we both examine our assumptions and conclusions with the clear eye of objective reason and recognize the emotions we have outgrown with the clear eye of the present heart. Because many of these habits of reasoning and emotion are holdovers from an earlier stage of our lives, however, they are easily mistaken for intrinsic aspects of ourselves. For this reason, it is often best to find an ally who has nothing to gain or lose by our decisions and with whom we can examine our reasoning and emotions. Where there are inconsistencies in our reasoning, we are using rationalizations to justify not disentangling ourselves; where past emotions are being triggered by present events, we remain entangled because we have not yet acknowledged the emotional progress we have achieved. When we come to terms with our own clear reasoning and present emotions, we can see through the entanglements of past decisions and recognize the decisions we must now make in order to extricate ourselves from difficulty. As difficult and time-consuming as this first stage of the process can be, the stage in which we actually implement our decisions to disentangle ourselves can require even greater effort and patience: It is essential that matters be ended well, at the right time and in the right way, or else we merely leap out of one entanglement and into another.

INTENT | The further we advance on the path of the spirit warrior, the more we honor this discipline of penetrating confusion. Every moment of our lives, indeed, is a confrontation with our own ability to distinguish between the real and illusion. To return to our true path from the least misstep, to correct every mistake before they can put forth seeds, to continually advance upon the goal of an untroubled, wise, and loving spirit—these are the facets of the diamond soul fashioned by the spirit warrior's own hands.

SUMMARY | Do not blame others. While some of these entanglements are not fair or reasonable, most of them result from decisions you made. While some of these problems could not be foreseen, most involved known risks you were warned about beforehand. Work patiently and methodically to disentangle yourself. Do not let the cost detract from the prize. Do not indulge self-pity.

The Line Changes

1ST   When people want to stand on the other shore without actually crossing the river, it is all just imagined progress. Resist your inclination to dabble in complex matters, acquiring only a taste of the full banquet. If this is really of interest to you, stop here and study it deeply for a long while.

2ND   When people are self-sacrificing out of loyalty and duty, they establish a precedent that inspires all around them. When your superior is wrongly attacked, resist any advice to save yourself. This is a partnership of mutual benefit—better to fall with the one who supported you than regret inaction.

3RD   The climate is changing—competition and self-promotion are inadvisable right now. What is needed of you at this time is consistent effectiveness and dependability. Resist the temptation to lead with your usual strength—develop a new demeanor that pleasantly surprises all around you.

4TH   When you have tried various approaches to advancing to the next level of influence and have been rebuffed at every turn, go back to square one and take up a new idea to develop. This allows you to fold your previous work into the new. Resist any loss of confidence—your time is coming.

5TH   Wave after wave of problems arise and, just as you are feeling overwhelmed, assistance comes from others who share your vision and values. Resist their efforts to downplay the significance of their help—display your sincere gratitude every chance you get. Your fortune is changed for the better.

6TH   Rain erodes the mountain, yet still it stands—weathered, but that merely reveals its character. The material hones the spiritual, yet still it is dull—sharper, but that merely reveals its potential. Everything below is an ally, awakening the higher from its daydream—resist spiritual drowsiness.

DISSOLVING
ARTIFICE

IMAGE | A male warrior sets down all his belongings and clothes and weapons and ritual objects and walks away into the wilderness, naked.

INTERPRETATION | The male warrior symbolizes the masculine creative force, who tests and trains human nature in order to increase its versatility and fortitude. That he sets aside all his belongings, clothes, weapons, and ritual objects means that you shed all you have relied upon, both in your relationship with other people and the divine, in order to arrive at your true sense of purpose. Walking away into the wilderness means that you return to that part of the world of experience that is still unknown and from which you received your original inspiration. That the warrior is naked means that nothing stands between you and the world of experience. Taken together, these symbols mean that you leave behind that with which you have been identified.

ACTION | The masculine half of the spirit warrior leaves behind goals and roles in search of the other half. It is easy to lose ourselves in our chosen pursuits, beliefs, and relationships. Despite being forewarned about such dangers, we end up trying to rediscover ourselves after a long interruption in our progress because our attention was captured by something that shaped how we felt about ourselves and how others felt about us. Losing ourselves in an activity or relationship is like falling into a trap that everyone talks about—we get used to it, cease to think about it, and then wonder how we could have overlooked such an obvious pitfall. Even those activities and relationships that are meaningful and positive cannot be mistaken for genuine fulfillment, since basing our identity on what we do or have means that our identity can be shattered as soon as what we do or have is taken from us. Though the head knows that seeking the other half of our true self elsewhere is dangerous, it is only when the heart recognizes the inside of the trap that we can escape. To search for the other half is to return to that place where there are no external pursuits, beliefs, or relationships. To walk away from what defines us is to step back to that place where we are quintessentially indefinable.

For this reason, it is a time for returning to the quest of experiencing the equally indefinable other half that mirrors the wilderness within you. Because your intent perfectly complements the other half's own quest, you find wholeness in that inner landscape where dwells the perfect complement to the living attention you have been cultivating all along.

INTENT | It is so easy to lose ourselves in our chosen pursuits, beliefs, and relationships because it seems for a time as if we have found who we truly are. Whether we are defined by conflict, pride, or acceptance, the energy moving through us seems an irresistible force sweeping us toward something fulfilling and important. Giving up the influence of that energy is not so easy—often we merely trade it for the energy we get from regret, anger, hurt, and despair. You are able to defeat such self-defeating energies because you train yourself to nurture every moment of creation with the living water of your attention. No longer finding yourself in the eyes of others, you set out to rediscover your unique relationship with all creation.

SUMMARY | Look forward with curiosity and a sense of exploration. Do not look backward with longing and a sense of regret. A wild animal released from captivity stays by its cage until it perceives it has been returned to freedom. No matter how secure the past seemed, it caged you into an artificial sense of who you are. No matter how unfamiliar the future appears, it is the road back to freedom.

THE LINE CHANGES

1ST   There is something very basic and fundamental deteriorating. Begin by checking your physical health, then that of those closest to you, then the state of things you depend on—foundation, roof, vehicle, appliances, and so forth. Don't procrastinate—prevent a major crisis by acting now.

2ND   Your loving-kindness and desire for intimacy are covered over by the memory of an old injury. But you cannot both protect your feelings and live life fully—this habit of armoring yourself was useful once but is now detrimental. You are strong enough now to risk suffering loss again.

3RD   When conditions around you are worsening, so that even your own position is in doubt, hold fast to the time-proven truths of your spiritual beliefs. Like an anchor securing you in rough seas, this connection sustains you when others would go under. This is the time to let your faith prove itself.

4TH   When people feel they give constantly but receive nothing in return, they become resentful and bitter, eventually poisoning the very well water they give others to drink. You must avoid this path at all costs. The inner must influence the outer, not the other way around.

5TH   As difficult as it is sometimes, by not showing favoritism you avoid the resentment and conflict that would tear the situation apart. Show each the same degree of familiarity, keep each at the same distance. You are wringing order out of disorder.

6TH   Sometimes it is best to have no apparent value. Imago cells serve no purpose in the caterpillar's life until they trigger the butterfly's metamorphosis. By holding fast to what others do not care about, you become the center around which the new is organized.

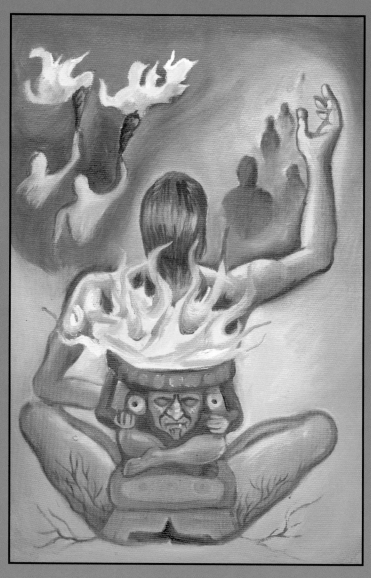

REVIVING
TRADITION

IMAGE | The ancient spirit of fire takes the form of a male warrior, who is made part of the land by the roots growing like veins through his body and the earth. His arm is raised, greeting the long line of people in shadow that approach him. Another line of people, their torches rekindled, depart in light.

INTERPRETATION | This hexagram depicts the ancestors' inheritance passing from individual to individual and from generation to generation. The ancient spirit of fire symbolizes the universal tradition of fire-making, whose timeless ritual unites all people in a common heritage. The male warrior symbolizes the self-discipline and training needed to stand against greed, ambition, and materialism. That he is made part of the land means that you find your spiritual home in the site of your own lifetime. The long line of people in shadow is a symbol of those seeking to find their way back to a balanced and harmonious way of life. The line of people departing with torches rekindled is a symbol of those who find the light of the ancestors inside their own hearts and carry it through the darkness of their own time. Taken together, these symbols mean that you resist spiritual erosion the way a mountain of righteousness stands against the wind of corruption and the rain of meaninglessness.

ACTION | The masculine half of the spirit warrior views everything as a buried treasure left behind by the spiritual ancestors for their descendants. It is a time for holding fast to what lasts rather than getting distracted by the novel or overwhelmed by the fleeting. Avoid participating in the fads and fashions of the day, seeking instead to uphold the values and world view of a more spiritual time. This means, first and foremost, respecting and honoring all that is not human. When matter is seen as devoid of spirit, then nature can be desecrated without a second thought; when one form of nature is seen as devoid of spirit, then all forms of life can be desecrated without a second thought; when one form of life is seen as devoid of spirit, then human beings can desecrate one another without a second thought. For this reason, the spirit warrior sees the world as the divine homeland shared by the living and the dead and those not yet born. Recognizing that meaningfulness is hidden from those who attack it, you look into the secret heart of things and see the One Spirit of creation everywhere you look. Recognizing that meaningfulness is an open secret to all but the greedy, ambitious, and materialistic, you bury the treasure again in your own turn so that your descendants will find their secret heart.

INTENT | Even though you feel out of step with the wounded spirit of the time, you are actively involved in healing it. Recognizing that its illness is meaninglessness, you feed it the medicine of meaningfulness day and night throughout your life. Just as the fire of light and warmth must be fed wood and air to continue burning, the spirit of the time must be fed the joy and insights born of meaningfulness if it is to continue living. Without the tradition of meaningful consecration to feed it, the spirit of the time will eventually die and be replaced by that of meaningless desecration. For this reason, the spirit warrior keeps alive the ancient tradition of training every thought and feeling to reflect the hidden sacredness of every moment.

SUMMARY | The more you put the world view of the ancients into practice, the more you have to offer others. Be generous with what you have learned but do not stop learning: Just as people depend on a well for their water, the well depends on the invisible river below ground for its water. Assume that you will understand matters better in the future and act with a corresponding degree of humility.

The Line Changes

1ST Take stock of those closest to you—what are their strengths, what are their weaknesses, how might you harm one another? Take this into account in all your actions and make your intentions clear in all your communications. With this as a basis, you can avoid any unnecessary rifts between allies.

2ND Take stock of those closest to you—what are their needs, what are their sorrows, how might you comfort one another? Take this into account in all your interactions. With this generosity of spirit as a basis, you can forge unbreakable bonds with each of your allies.

3RD The alliance is splitting into two camps—one where discipline is too strict and the other, too lenient. When conduct is too severe, members find fault everywhere—when too frivolous, members do not even question their own effectiveness. Get rid of extremists on both sides and restore the balance.

4TH Ethics emerge from bad judgment—they are the collective memory of what does not benefit the whole. Those who work together to serve others must encourage one another to maintain humility and respect at all times, even in private. Without the proper attitude, servants become masters.

5TH Principles emerge from ethics—they are the collective memory of what is worth striving for. Peace is achieved when leaders are content and sincere—prosperity is achieved when leaders do not concentrate the wealth. Nothing holds people together better than sustained peace and prospering.

6TH Wisdom emerges from principles—it is the collective memory of what produces happiness. Those who evaluate their own conduct, building on their successes and correcting their faults, dwell together in shared well-being. This is the road of freedom that leads to the ecstatic life.

ADAPTING
EXPERIENCE

IMAGE | A spider waits for its quarry to fall prey to the design of its web. The web is constructed in the empty space between two branches to catch unwary insects mistaking it for a natural passageway through which to fly.

INTERPRETATION | This hexagram depicts the art of learning. The spider symbolizes natural skill, calm patience, and creative adaptability. That it waits for its quarry to fly into its web means that you wait for *benefit* to seek you rather than you seeking it. The design of the web symbolizes a perfect and unchanging model of effectiveness that must constantly be adapted and changed to fit the circumstances at hand. That the web is constructed in an empty space that can be mistaken for a natural passageway means that the best trap looks like the best opportunity. Taken together, these symbols mean that you continue to make progress by learning how to better surprise yourself with every new experience.

ACTION | The spirit warrior does not allow past successes to interfere with learning. It is a mistake to look at new experiences solely in the light of past experience. To see each new moment merely as an extension of what has come before blinds us to the ongoing act of creation making the universe anew every moment. In this sense, the more we learn, the more prone we are to view things according to what we have learned—and when our new experiences merely serve to reinforce what we already know, then learning effectively stops and we are guided by our expectations. The spider can never spin the same web twice. Branches grow and move, leaves sprout and fall off, the wind comes and goes, the seasons pass and return, a web that ensnares an insect must be repaired or replaced, the spider moves to another tree or bush. That which we seek, that which we need for nourishment, that by which we learn and grow and create, that which we call understanding, eludes us until we turn all we have learned to an exploration of the new and unexpected in every experience. In order to have new experiences, then, we learn to experience life in new ways—if we are to trap the quarry of ever-evolving learning and growth and creativity, then we must use those strands of learning, growth, and creativity to weave an ever-evolving way of seeing and knowing the world as the newborn creation it truly is. What is true for the world is also true for ourselves: The sum of all our body's experiences must not be mistaken for our immortal newborn spirit.

INTENT | It is best to use what you know as a foundation from which to start over with something completely new. There is more progress to be made by exploring new aspects of long-standing endeavors than by trying to complete them in their existing form. Watch your reactions and listen to your thoughts, encouraging the creative and insightful ones while discouraging the automatic and habitual. Avoid falling prey to others' traps. Be especially wary of new opportunities that offer sudden wealth, success, recognition, or influence. Real advancement can be had by adapting all your skill and knowledge to the task of creating a clearing in your life where *benefit* can accumulate to meet the *need* of the greatest number.

SUMMARY | Although the skills and strategies you have learned in life can be successfully adapted to present circumstances, it is the skills and strategies you have not yet learned that hold the keys to your real happiness. Don't simply rely on what has worked before. If you are not getting the reactions you want, then keep changing what you are doing until you do. Experiment and thrive.

THE LINE CHANGES

1ST In dealing with people whose animal nature is not yet tamed, first assess whether their moment of metamorphosis is at hand. Except in the rare cases where it is, present nothing interesting that might catch their attention. Save your energy for those open to change.

2ND In dealing with partners, be like acrobats who are continuously making slight adjustments to keep in balance with each other's smallest movements. Provide a counterbalance to the other's extremes. Communicate closely and often about shared values and visions so no negative influence may enter.

3RD In dealing with people in the workplace, do not form cliques or engage in power struggles. Neither give offense nor take offense—make it easy for others to get along with you. Work to make your reactions more consistent and predictable—allow people to count on you and all will go well.

4TH In dealing with those above and below, it is not enough to merely be effective—you must spend time cultivating relationships, especially with those below, otherwise people imagine your interests lie elsewhere. Enjoy being more social. Without the confidence of both, you can serve neither.

5TH In dealing with leading others, you must be able to adjust your thinking to the circumstances at hand—do not lead people over the cliff of ideology. Elicit advice from all sides—do not cater to any faction whatsoever. Lead with humility and the highest ethics.

6TH In dealing with exile, first entertain no nostalgia about the past. Then, stay focused on your long-range goals but intersperse your efforts with new avenues of study and new experiences. This can be the most meaningful time of your life if you keep learning, evolving, and leaning forward.

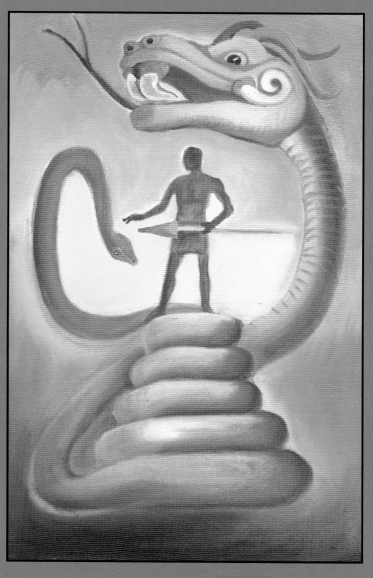

FEIGNING
COMPLIANCE

IMAGE | A shadowy male warrior stands upon the coils of a great serpent, forcing it to submit to his will at spear point. He has, however, mistaken the snake's tail for its head, which rises above and behind him, ready to strike.

INTERPRETATION | The shadowy male warrior symbolizes those who seek to dominate others. The point of the spear symbolizes force, whether in the form of aggression, threat, intimidation, or subversion. The great serpent symbolizes the energy and power of those who resist domination. Its coils symbolize the convolutions and intricacies of the strategy of invisible defiance. That the serpent's tail is shaped to look like its head means that you are able to disguise your true intent behind a mask of conformity. That the serpent's head is poised to strike means that you remain vigilant, neither missing any real opportunity for resistance nor getting lulled into a false sense of security. Taken together, these symbols mean that you lull your captor into a false sense of security while awaiting the right moment to reclaim your freedom.

ACTION | There is no true victory in force, because those who have been overcome eventually use the moral high ground to achieve their independence. Such a turn of events is made inevitable by the fact that the spirit of those who oppress is progressively sickened by their past actions at just the time that the spirit of those oppressed is made progressively stronger and finer by the hardship they have endured. Force corrupts those who use it and ennobles those who endure it. For this reason, those who use force fail because they are brutish and short-sighted while those whose spirit cannot be dominated succeed because they are humane and wise. When those who are stronger seek to dominate and control us then we must develop a strategy that ensures we defeat our oppressors without repeating their mistakes. In this sense, it is necessary that we commit beforehand to making no attempt to exact revenge from those who have wronged us. In order to emerge unscathed from domination we have to recognize the indomitable nature we have inherited from our ancestors and then ally ourselves with others committed to preserving inner independence until outer independence can be openly celebrated. Because you take the time to gather inner strength without arousing any suspicion, you succeed in freeing yourself without harming another. Because your humaneness shines on your oppressors, you succeed in freeing them without harming yourself.

INTENT | The spirit warrior refrains from attempting to dominate anyone in any way, for fear of the inevitable and justifiable backlash it would produce. Others are not necessarily so farsighted, however: At a time when force and intimidation are openly used to control our actions and shape our attitudes, it is imperative that we train ourselves to resist every tendency to succumb to mental or spiritual tyranny. By adopting a demeanor of naive complacency while making our true thoughts and feelings unreadable, we make it possible to live with oppression without being conquered by it. Using visible compliance to mask invisible defiance, we maintain our reverence toward all things so that we never wrong others the way we were wronged.

SUMMARY | When those who are more powerful demand you submit to their will, do not just pretend to go along with them—make a show of agreeing with them and working for their goals as if they were your own. Keep your true feelings to yourself, work to find kindred spirits who can be trusted, and gather your strength until the moment to reclaim your independence and freedom arrives.

THE LINE CHANGES

1ST Many around you exercise no self-control and seem resigned to wandering purposelessly through life. Though you empathize with them, do not allow them to hold you back. Look to others outside your current sphere as examples of what you wish to be—train to acquire the skills you will need.

2ND The most profound relationships cannot be anticipated—support and acceptance come from an unlikely source. Grief gives way to gratitude, anxiety gives way to enthusiasm—your hard work and good works bring you recognition. Study the successes of your predecessors for inspiration.

3RD Prove your dedication to those around you and they see your advance as their own—earn their trust and they propel you forward. This is a difficult position, remaining true to your peers and adapting to the needs of those above, but you manage it well. Just be a conduit and communicate clearly.

4TH When people enter into a cause for the wrong reason, they will perceive ethical standards to be rules filled with intentional loopholes. The bigger the decisions you make, the less you can try to take advantage of loopholes. Personal gain must be completely set aside—work for the common good.

5TH Experienced people understand that success and failure depend more on circumstances than personal ability. Simply do your best in fulfilling your responsibilities—regardless of the outcome, your efforts will enhance your reputation. This project will lead to a more important one.

6TH When people do not recognize their own essence, they do not recognize the essence of others. This is the path of repression and aloneness. Look for the self-sameness inherent in everyone—self-importance and comparing yourself to others is not the road of freedom.

INTERPRETING
INSIGHT

IMAGE | Seated on a reed mat at the edge of the wilderness, a female warrior paints the sun and moon. Using the red and black paint and tree bark paper of the old ones, she depicts the sun as an eagle and the moon as a jaguar.

INTERPRETATION | The woven mat symbolizes the old ones' way of life, for they were born on the mat and took their meals on the mat and slept on the mat and were married on the mat and conceived their children on the mat and were buried in the mat. The female warrior symbolizes the feminine creative force, who conceives in order to nurture and sustain what is valuable. That she sits at the edge of the wilderness means that you set aside time, apart from other people and the routines of everyday life, to both discover and give form to your own personal vision. The sun and moon symbolize the primordial halves of the universal duality, whose opposing halves complement one another in order to unite in a greater whole. Both the red and black paint and the paper made from tree bark are symbols of the old ones' wisdom and artistry. That she depicts the sun as an eagle and the moon as a jaguar means that you give new form to old meanings, thereby rooting your vision in the old ones' vision even as you keep theirs alive through your own. Taken together, these symbols mean that you find your own way to give voice to the timeless longings of unchanging human nature.

ACTION | The feminine half of the spirit warrior searches for the unforeseen relationships between things. It is a time for looking closely at the course of change and determining how it threatens the ideals of freedom and justice and equality. If those who can see through obfuscation and misdirection do not act in a timely manner to preserve the valuable, then who will seize the opportunity to prevent wider suffering? Of special concern is any tendency toward accepting authoritarianism, since it would signal that those using fear to dominate others were close to achieving victory. Because you possess the insight to penetrate the fog of words surrounding ulterior motives, it falls to you to express your vision of truth and illusion in a manner that draws allies together in the battle against the abuse of power. Because you possess the insight to penetrate the fog of rationalizations surrounding greed and ambition, it falls to you to give new form to the ancient symbols of the spirit of the living duality in a manner that draws allies together in the battle against the glorification of materialism. Just as our study of nature draws ever subtler lessons from the hidden relationships we uncover, the study of human nature shows how we can apply those lessons to mastering the tides of cooperation and competition forever ebbing and flowing between people. Because you incorporate the ancient into your endeavor to preserve the worthwhile, the forms you use to express your vision resonate with others' visions and influence the orientation and timing of their own endeavors. Because you incorporate the ancient way of life into your own, you succeed by alternating the intent of your actions between change and stability, between daring and caution, in accord with your surroundings.

INTENT | Insight comes from experiencing surprising relationships between things. Interpretation comes from creating surprising relationships between things. If we experience the sun radiating light like spirit and the moon reflecting light like the senses, then equating the eagle with the sun and the jaguar with the moon may be said to mean that spirit is that which sees far in light and the senses are that which see far in darkness. If we further experience the sun and moon as two halves of a single creative force revealing itself in the cyclic alternation of day and night, then equating the eagle with spirit and the jaguar with the senses may be said to mean that the spirit warrior is whole and complete when one eye sees far into the world of light and the other eye sees far into the world of darkness. By keeping alive the dynamic tension inherent to the universal duality, we unite our masculine and feminine halves, thereby continuing this wondrous creation born from the ecstatic union of the great father and great mother.

SUMMARY | Whether expressing your love for nature, humanity, or the divine, you reflect a truth that shines beneath the blinding surface of appearances. Take care to be fooled neither by your opponents nor your allies. Question your willingness to believe others, continue pushing yourself to experience things firsthand. Use the element of surprise to call people's attention to your endeavor.

The Line Changes

1ST   This is not a good time to make a move—your resources are not yet sufficient to see you all the way through to the end. Avoid making decisions based on others' vision of trends. Wait until you feel yourself pulled in the direction of your long-held passions and values.

2ND   Others around you grow impatient—they find fault with you and try to persuade you to go along with them. Some stay, some leave, and some come back—take none of this personally, for they are acting out their own inner conflicts. Be reassuring but do not try to persuade anyone of anything.

3RD   You decide to go ahead despite advice and warnings to the contrary. In the face of bad odds, you believe you can prevail—go ahead if you must but try to improve your chances of success by using the utmost caution, foresight, flexibility, and mobility. You cannot be too prepared.

4TH   Trying to please others, you put yourself at risk—trying to direct events, you create danger for yourself. The fact that there are no hard and fast rules in life means that you must forge your own and live by them. Do not depart from your established priorities.

5TH   You have made an island of calm where you can ride out this storm of turbulent times. Stay put, making yourself available to those close to you—collude with no one but offer advice to those who come seeking it. You are not expendable and so are not in danger of losing your position.

6TH   The difficulty seems inescapable—you have run out of options and have every reason to fear the worst. Keep your motives pure and your conduct beyond reproach—assistance will arrive in time to avoid disaster. Maintain your faith and outlook—others will adopt your vision as their own.

GOING
BEYOND

IMAGE | A male warrior, wearing an elaborate headdress of masks, walks the road of stars. The innermost mask is that of a skeleton, from which emerge masks of a young man, an old man, and another skeleton. Crowned with a crest of precious feathers of the quetzal bird, the entire headdress is bound together by the rope the warrior holds in his hands. The stars are drawn as the eyes of night in order to show that the ancestors watch over us even as we dream.

INTERPRETATION | This hexagram depicts the will to cross every threshold. The male warrior symbolizes the masculine creative force, who tests and trains human nature in order to increase its versatility and fortitude. The road of stars symbolizes the spirit's journey through the universe of lifetimes. The headdress of masks symbolizes the great cycle of metamorphosis passing from death to birth, through youth, old age, and back again to death. The crest of quetzal feathers symbolizes the sacred nature of the spirit warrior's metamorphosis. The rope tying the headdress together symbolizes the thread of immortal awareness running through the eternity of lifetimes. The warrior holding the ends of the rope means that it is the present lifetime which knots the rope of eternity together. That the stars shine in the darkness like the ancestors' watchful guidance means that you follow in the footsteps of other indomitable spirits. Taken together, these symbols mean that you move through lifetimes with practiced ease, accomplishing each lifetime's objective with unstudied grace.

ACTION | The masculine half of the spirit warrior follows the road of transcendence past every destination. By challenging ourselves to better embody the characteristics of outer flexibility and inner strength, we neither seek to control externals nor allow ourselves to be controlled by externals. By denying externals the power to influence our reactions and feelings, we transform that power into spiritual freedom and autonomy. In this sense, we stop our attention from leaking, accumulate its power, and then convert it into the spiritual freedom to move easily between diverse activities and the spiritual autonomy to remain unmoved by gain or loss. When we can be neither distracted nor unnerved by externals, then we are neither led forward by longings nor pushed backward by disappointments. By keeping attention focused on the present moment of attention itself, in other words, we prevent our actions and emotions from being influenced by either encouragement or discouragement from the outside. Adapting to circumstances without being possessed by them, unmoved by circumstances without losing affection for them—such is the path of transcendence the spirit warrior walks in order to bring *benefit* to others without any thought of self. Because you act on the knowledge that circumstances are not happening to you but, rather, around you, this is a time in which all obstacles are overcome and all goals exceeded.

INTENT | Nothing can hold us back if we cultivate heartfelt curiosity about the limits of our own awareness. It is this curiosity that propels us to seek out the time-tested teachings of our spiritual ancestors and to train ourselves to extend our sphere of awareness further into the world beyond the senses. By becoming more aware of our true surroundings, we are able to perceive the unfulfilled *need* that everywhere continues to thwart real advancement. By not becoming self-satisfied or complacent, we continue to expand the limits of our awareness, discovering thereby the *benefit* needed to fulfill the *need* at hand. Because you treat this world as if it were already the next, you are able to use the laws of spiritual cause-and-effect to help advance the spiritual metamorphosis of the current generation another stage.

SUMMARY | Your will power is growing stronger, take care not to place limits on your thinking. Do not be satisfied with your ambitions. Push past the goals you have in mind, begin to believe that you are capable of much more than you can imagine. Nothing is holding you back right now but your own thinking. Begin to believe that you are much more than you can imagine. You are entering a time of long-awaited success.

THE LINE CHANGES

1ST The window of opportunity opens—the pivot of constructive change is in the palm of your hand. Look at your own era as if for the first time and adapt the perennial message to the needs of the time. The season has arrived and the soil is prepared—yours is the role of sowing the seeds of light.

2ND Without genuine affection for the unfortunate, it is impossible to feel benevolent—only uncontrived generosity and altruistic good will allow you to reach your full potential. Open your heart to the suffering of others. This is the way to deepen a river that is already conspicuous for its breadth.

3RD When people are excitable and social by nature, they keep making the same type of mistakes over and over. Then their good-heartedness brings them back to self-awareness and a commitment to not repeating those mistakes again. Learn from such people and avoid this path of restlessness.

4TH No one is more surprised than an immoral person when lightning strikes and they suddenly acquire morality. You must not give up on others just because they have not yet changed for the better—it is impossible to predict what people will become. Expect the best of everyone.

5TH Perfection is a process of becoming, an evolutionary momentum directed at limitless improvement. Your will to perfect yourself makes you sincere, modest, and willing to correct your faults without any rationalization. How can you not attain your heart's desire?

6TH The window of opportunity closes—there will be no more warnings. Despite repeated chances to reform yourself, you are sinking back into self-destructive habits of thought and feeling. If you don't undergo a change of heart now, you will initiate a long period of darkness and confusion.

44

REFINING
INSTINCT

IMAGE | A male warrior places all his weapons and shields into a fire, the smoke from which takes the form of an ethereal butterfly.

INTERPRETATION | The male warrior symbolizes the testing and training that make people more adaptable, inventive, and courageous. That he burns up all his weapons and shields means that you eliminate every tendency to attack others or defend yourself. The fire symbolizes the inner work whereby old habits of thought, feeling, and behavior are converted into conscious acts of self-expression. That the smoke takes the form of a butterfly means that your new habits of thought, feeling, and behavior reflect the spiritual metamorphosis you have undertaken. Taken together, these symbols mean that you voluntarily subordinate your personal desires to a higher purpose.

ACTION | The masculine half of the spirit warrior uses the energy of the meaningless to give form to the meaningful. At the core of the spirit warrior's intent is the wholehearted effort to stop wasting energy. Such an effort is futile so long as we succumb to the impulse to divide our experiences into opportunities and threats—opportunities to gain some advantage over others and threats of others taking advantage of us. From the spirit warrior's perspective, we waste energy until we stop obeying the base and brutish drives to exploit the vulnerabilities of others and block others from exploiting ours. When we are devoid of any hope for gain or any fear of loss, all the energy of those baser impulses is available to be used for higher aims. In other words, when the goals of baser motives lose their meaning, their energy can be transferred to new goals whose nobler motives imbue them with a sense of genuine meaningfulness. Harnessing base energy and directing it toward nobler goals is, in itself, the act of conserving energy. Voluntarily placing the baser instincts in the service of nobler goals is, in itself, the act of refining the instincts. The emergence of our refined instincts is then embodied in the desire to express our vision in creative acts that bring *benefit* to people, nature, and spirit. Because you voluntarily moderate the way in which you express your vision, you do not provoke an angry and oppressive backlash against your cause. Because you do not give others ammunition to use against your endeavor, it succeeds by moving past all resistance. By not thinking in terms of personal gain and loss, you are able to act in accord with your highest ideals, make allies of those with similar values, and work together to realize your common goals.

INTENT | We spiritualize desire when we stop wasting energy on the pursuit of meaningless desires—those that either cannot be attained or, if attained, ultimately prove unfulfilling. Likewise, we spiritualize the instincts when we stop wasting energy on the pursuit of base instincts—those that give rise to meaningless desires. By spiritualizing the instincts, we follow in the footsteps of those who have created the most sublime monuments to the human spirit. Because your spiritual instincts give rise to meaningful desires, you use the transformed energy of the meaningless to both give form to the meaningful and bring *benefit* to the people, nature, and spirit touching your life.

SUMMARY | Identify the goals you pursue out of fear, greed, or the need for approval—then make a conscious decision to no longer pursue those goals. Create a new set of goals based on trust, generosity, and giving others the approval they deserve—then make a conscious decision to pursue those goals. Be strict with yourself: Do not allow yourself to unconsciously slip back into pursuing your old goals. You are your longings.

THE LINE CHANGES

1ST Long-standing tensions do not resolve overnight—though the direction and momentum of change are both positive, its pace is slower than you wish. If you want peace outside, you must practice it inside—go along with the pace of change, not against it. Things are still cold and dim at sunrise.

2ND The window of opportunity opens—your relationship blossoms with renewed delight. The factors that have caused such distress are finally seen for the mirages they are—together you ignore them in favor of the oasis right before you. The affection you revel in today is tomorrow's devotion.

3RD In the course of performing your duties, you repeatedly exaggerate the importance of your position. You have neither the strength nor the backing to hold on to it, however, so now others can take it away from you if they want it. Before you speak or act, ask yourself, what can go wrong?

4TH An associate you like personally turns out to be as unscrupulous as people say. Regardless of your feelings, you can no longer associate with this person. The minor damage to your reputation can still be repaired but you must be more careful to associate with people who have impeccable ethics.

5TH In a sea of bureaucracy, you are an island of authenticity. Surrounded by those who accept its dehumanizing practices, you are a voice of true reason. Changing people's long-standing attitudes will be difficult, though—it is best to add new people with the right outlook as opportunity permits.

6TH The search for peace of mind can itself become a source of anxiety and dissatisfaction. And it can lead to all kinds of questionable pursuits. The cornerstone of the inner sanctum is sincerity—if your heart is truly filled with the profound desire to find peace, then nothing can stand in your way.

CASTING
OFF

IMAGE | An ancient spirit, part man, part bird, and part serpent, sheds its skin and takes flight.

INTERPRETATION | This hexagram depicts achieving freedom from the past. The man is a symbol of the training and self-discipline that leads to a harmonious and balanced lifetime. The bird is a symbol of spirit, whose vision comes from the sky. The serpent is a symbol of the body, whose vision comes from the earth. Taken together, this ancient spirit symbolizes the unified and integrated nature of the masculine half of the spirit warrior. That it sheds its skin and takes flight means that you leave behind what you have outgrown and take up the challenge of a more ennobling way of life. Taken together, these symbols mean that your training and self-discipline free you from living a life defined by others.

ACTION | The masculine half of the spirit warrior sheds the old self. As difficult as it sometimes is to believe ourselves capable of thinking new thoughts, feeling new emotions, and experiencing the world in new and more joyous ways, the time comes when all our planting, pruning, and cultivating bears just that fruit. Just as continuous pressure inevitably transforms coal into diamond, continuous effort to purify awareness inevitably transforms the troubled spirit into the untroubled spirit—and, just as the change from coal to diamond is permanent and irreversible, so too is the metamorphosis of the troubled spirit into the untroubled spirit. Although many people express a desire to permanently transform themselves, few are willing to apply themselves on a moment-to-moment, day-to-day, basis. Because they make half-hearted attempts instead of continuously concentrating on purifying the present moment of awareness, they resign themselves to the status quo and dismiss others' efforts to achieve real freedom as futile. For this reason, it takes self-reliance and endurance to achieve a true change of heart. It is impossible to leave behind our past sense of self until we leave behind the way those around us define human nature and its potential. Rather than being worn down by the conformity all around us, we use the troubled words and actions of others as the whetstone against which we scrape away all but the untroubled spirit. It is a time for having faith in your capacity to transform yourself. Because your spirit has not been broken by adversity or disillusion, it emerges from the past purified and serene: Nothing more stands between you and freedom but that you see the chains are broken and have fallen away from your feet.

INTENT | The untroubled spirit is untroubled even when things are difficult, the troubled spirit is troubled even when things are going well. Conscientiously watching our own habits of thought and feeling as we react to things, we are able to achieve greater inner balance by stopping bad habits and continuing good ones. Likewise, conscientiously watching our actions toward nature, people, and spirit, we are able to achieve greater outer harmony by stopping harmful actions and continuing beneficial ones. Consistently striving to reach this union of inner balance and outer harmony enables us to cast off that which is dark and heavy and become that which is bright and light. In this sense, brightness is the quality of contentment and joy that the untroubled spirit radiates, whereas lightness is the quality of ease and buoyancy of the untroubled spirit's presence. Because you diligently cultivate peace of mind, you shed every last vestige of agitation, restlessness, and uneasiness.

SUMMARY | See the thoughts and feelings that drag you down as habits you have outgrown. Treat them like bad habits you acquired in the past and set your mind to breaking them now. The time is especially auspicious for such an effort. The freedom and happiness you have always sought is within reach. When you clearly see that others have different habits of thought and feeling than you do, then you know you can change yourself and stop believing that you are your habits.

THE LINE CHANGES

1ST   You gather people around you based on proximity, not talent—they can learn to follow instruction but cannot advise you about what to do next. This allows them to advance further than they had hoped, so they are most loyal. Your own loyalty to them makes your benevolence apparent to all.

2ND   Someone in your midst is chronically dissatisfied, disrupting your own peace of mind but not that of those loyal to you. Able to forgive, if not to forget, you give this person a second chance to be part of the endeavor. Your flexibility and affection make your benevolence apparent to all.

3RD   The one chronically dissatisfied betrays your trust a second time—you cannot afford to treat matters with either wishful thinking or despair. You have to make a clean break, letting the past go. Difficult as the decision is personally, it assures your future happiness and success.

4TH   You gather people around you based on talent, not proximity—they are able to advise you on the next stage of your journey. The dark cloud overshadowing your blessings begins to dissipate and you begin looking to the future again. Worry has led you to peace of mind.

5TH   Establishing endeavors and setting up trustworthy people to manage them, you build one success upon another, benefiting others and thereby yourself. Giving them the freedom and responsibility to manage their part earns you their respect and loyalty. Benevolence has led you to happiness.

6TH   You look to posterity, seeking a way to share the blessings and lessons life has bestowed on you. You focus your attention inwardly, looking for the source of attention—you focus your motivation inwardly, looking for the source of motivation. Contemplation has led you to the further shore.

HONORING
CONTENTMENT

IMAGE | A female warrior receives the affection of her grandson.

INTERPRETATION | This hexagram depicts the source of contentment. The female warrior symbolizes the feminine creative force, who conceives in order to nurture and sustain what is valuable. Her grandson symbolizes the extended family of all our loved ones, all our friends, all our relations. That she receives her grandson's affection means that you open your heart to the overflowing joy abiding in the eternal moment of love unreservedly shared. Taken together, these symbols mean that you increasingly find meaning and power in acts of simple and unadorned affection.

ACTION | The feminine half of the spirit warrior embodies the wellspring of blessings. Just as that which is truly loved is truly nurtured and that which is truly nurtured truly grows greater, that which receives blessings is destined to dispense them. Only those who feel wholehearted gratitude for the blessings borne by ordinary and everyday circumstances are able to give others the kind of pure and unselfish love that truly nurtures greatness. True greatness is greatness of spirit, just as true love is love of another's spirit. If we wish to encourage others, we must reflect the loving-kindness that shines upon us. It is a time, in other words, for more than simply feeling content—it is a time for honoring our contentment by directing our joy into gratitude for the blessings bestowed by the divine unseen forces. Sanctifying the love we share with those in front of us helps crystallize the love we share with those behind us. Allowing ourselves to be loved by those we can see teaches us to allow ourselves to be loved by those we cannot see. It is to our spiritual ancestors that we turn, then, when we honor contentment, for it is in the company of the ancestors that we find our home. Because we are destined to eventually become one of the ancestors, it is only natural that we come to be better able to sense the love, care, and guidance they give us every moment. Dwelling in the deep and abiding sense of fulfillment that comes with loving and being loved, therefore, makes us better able to see the spirit of our loved ones and understand how to nurture the greatness of each. In this, we repeat what we learned from those who truly saw our spirit and truly nurtured its greatness. It is in this manner that everyday moments of pure, unselfish love are transformed into bridges that span all the generations, binding them together in the single act of universal love.

INTENT | The continuity that binds the generations together arises from the meaning and power of the memories each of us make of our experiences—and the meaning and power of each memory arises from the emotions and insights we possess while in the midst of its experience. For this reason, there are few actions we can take that are more significant and beneficial than honoring contentment. In this sense, contentment means that you wholeheartedly experience the joy of being a loving part of a loving universe, whereas honoring means that you see spirit within every form and nurture its metamorphosis. Toward this end the spirit warrior trains to love every thing in creation as though it were a grandchild.

SUMMARY | Recognize moments when you are content. Recognize moments when you are at peace. Recognize moments when you feel love. Do not let these moments pass unnoted: Share them with spirit and thank spirit for its blessings and vow to spirit that you will work hard to deserve many more such moments. Be good company for spirit and you swim in the sea of bliss.

THE LINE CHANGES

1ST   When circumstances get the better of people, long-suffering courage gives way to hopelessness. You must fight your way out of this morass—to just stay here will allow matters to worsen. Force yourself to exercise and eat better—then find a place to volunteer and help others less fortunate.

2ND   When people are fortunate enough to have companionship and security, they can become self-satisfied and then stop growing. It is one thing to celebrate good fortune and another to sink into mere gratification of the senses. Always support the best in each other, not the worst.

3RD   When people are given a futile task, they take it to heart and allow it to affect their self-confidence. Once you appreciate that it is infinitely better to fail at a futile task than an achievable one, you will regain your composure. Bring out your flexible half again—this is a test of character, not ability.

4TH   When people are haunted by old wrongs, they keep returning to the memory in hope of laying it to rest—but peace of mind seems to take forever to arrive. Your commitment to untying this old knot is finally rewarded and you bring this misery to an end. There is no reason to revisit it ever again.

5TH   When leaders are unable to fulfill the expectations placed on them, they are publicly humiliated. If you accept blame without shifting it to others or making any excuses, then those above and below forgive you and allow you a fresh start. Your honesty and sincerity bring benefit to all eventually.

6TH   When circumstances overwhelm people with unforeseeable changes, sensible cautiousness gives way to paralysis. You cannot hold on to what is valuable by refusing to act—introspect here and see where this timidity began. Make a decision now that excites you about the future.

MAKING
INDIVIDUAL

IMAGE | At the edge of the rain forest, a male warrior wearing a jaguar necklace gazes into a mirror from which smoke arises. Within the smoking mirror, the warrior's reflection takes the form of a jaguar.

INTERPRETATION | This hexagram depicts the individual who both steps outside the flow of the generations and unites them. The male warrior symbolizes the way of testing and training human nature that increases its versatility and fortitude. The jaguar necklace symbolizes your true self united with the lineage of spiritual ancestors and living descendants. The smoking mirror symbolizes the work of self-reflection required to see through all our roles and pretenses in order to see our true self. That his reflection takes the form of a jaguar means that the true self blends into its surroundings so as to avoid drawing attention to its actual movements. That he stands at the edge of the rain forest means that the encounter with the true self occurs spontaneously and naturally once the desert of aloneness and self-discipline has been crossed. Taken together, these symbols mean that you embody the true self, free of artifice, self-interest, or compulsions.

ACTION | The masculine half of the spirit warrior steps out of the stream of evolution in order to divert it back into its original course. When we see the great work of the first creative forces to give spirit a form in matter and then in life and then in consciousness, we bear witness to the vast stretch of time that enfolds the world in the first ancestors' vision: Out of the single original act of creation arises this form before our eyes that continues to come ever closer to reflecting its formless spirit. But even as the world of form moves toward more perfectly expressing the world of spirit, its evolution is continually threatened by forms that gain dominance through the imbalances and disharmony they create. Because they divert the great work from its original course of evolution, the influence of these destructive forms must continually be counteracted by the influence of those creating balance and harmony. It is impossible, however, to identify these destructive forms of matter, life, or consciousness with certainty during the course of one's lifetime since it is only from the vantage point of history that such conclusions can be reached. For this reason, we do not react against other forms based on our own judgments and preferences. We act, rather, from the perspective of the true self, whose only goal is universal evolution toward perfection. Although the true self is inherent within every individual, it is dormant and dreamlike until we fully awaken to its presence—until we fully awaken to the presence of spirit in this matter, this life, this consciousness. Such awakenings of the true self, whose essential nature is the same everywhere, are how individuals become able to step out of the stream of evolution and know spontaneously and naturally the proper actions to help bring it back to its original course. Now is the time for considering the grand scope of creation and the place your actions have in it. It is not necessary to force decisions—simply pursue self-knowledge, put it into daily practice, and follow the true self's vision. Let go others' opinions and you succeed beyond measure.

INTENT | To be an individual means, in part, to no longer be unduly influenced by others—a state that is attained by stripping away all the social conditioning we have accepted since birth. But this state merely initiates true individuality, which is fashioned from all the subsequent decisions we make on our own. In particular, the sense of responsibility for others, as well as the deep-seated desire for companionship and community, appear to be essential values of the true self. Consciously deciding to pursue the goals and values of the true self means that we continue to do many of the things we did before awakening to its presence—we just do them differently. We act with a higher purpose in mind, we derive a deeper meaning from our experiences, and we bring a greater quality of *benefit* to the lives of others. In this way, true individuals are more profoundly a part of their surroundings than those in whom the true self yet dreams.

SUMMARY | Reflect on the choices you have been making recently. Observe how they have been adding up to something not quite defined and leading you in an unforeseen direction. Look at these choices as soul decisions forging your unique destiny. See yourself as your soul sees you—how is this lifetime of yours different from all others? Of all the flowers in the world, why this one?

THE LINE CHANGES

1ST   The window of opportunity opens—from the very beginning you display all the signs of one intent on accomplishing great things. You are an intrinsic part of the times and perfectly attuned to the needs and drives of your contemporaries. Take care to balance your intellect with loving-kindness.

2ND   Your strong will and mercurial temperament are tempered by the self-sacrificing character of your loved ones. Learning generosity and patience from these relationships, you cultivate a sincere demeanor of humility. Those closest to you are proud of your shining character.

3RD   It is your instinct to press ahead with this opportunity even though it means a leap into unknown waters. For some reason, this complete departure from past experience seems natural and right. This is the sense of discovery and adventure that makes your future accomplishments inevitable.

4TH   Fascinated with learning new things in order to help others, you gain the trust and confidence of all. It is easy to lose one's humility in the heady air of success, so keep your feet on the ground and hold firm to ethical conduct every moment. Do not expect everyone to be as ambitious as you.

5TH   Your inclination to be as critical of others as you are of yourself is tempered by the support and loyalty of your allies. Where others might stumble beneath the weight of responsibilities, you redouble your efforts. In this way your cultivated character becomes as great as your innate talents.

6TH   Do not rest on your past accomplishments—although the hour seems late, your most meaningful work lies ahead. With the help of strong allies, the pinnacle of your monument pierces the highest clouds. Helping people clear away long-standing ills, you are bathed in the glow of homecoming.

MOVING
SOURCE

IMAGE | An ancient spirit, part woman and part river, flows joyfully across the land. The water that splashes from the river takes on the form of jade spirit helpers. The waves and currents of the river are drawn as jade beads and speech glyphs and small conch shells.

INTERPRETATION | This hexagram depicts the living edge of renewal. The woman symbolizes that which gives birth and nourishes life. The river symbolizes the ever-changing flow of creation that persists in its never-changing direction. Taken together, this ancient spirit symbolizes spirit's never-changing love for life's ever-changing journey. The jade spirit helpers symbolize the unseen forces who nourish and enrich all they touch. The jade beads and speech glyphs and small conch shells symbolize the precious nature of the ever-renewing song of that single force which benefits all life and spirit. Taken together, these symbols mean that you bring *benefit* to others by responding to the headlong rush of events with spontaneity, daring, and creativity.

ACTION | The feminine half of the spirit warrior adapts to change with the ease and fluidity of running water. Life continually creates, renewing itself every moment, keeping the world forever fresh and new. By learning from nature how to move through the seasons of springtime birth, wintertime death, and springtime rebirth, we come to dwell on the living edge of renewal. The wisdom of the creative forces reveals itself most clearly in the way that things can endure and attain great age by maintaining their living edge of renewal. By adopting this strategy as their way of life, spirit warriors move the living source of renewal through the landscape of their lifetimes and the generations. Such wisdom is based on the essential nature of the creative forces, whose masculine half creates discovery and exploration and whose feminine half creates enjoyment and fulfillment—a duality whose union of curiosity and playfulness reveals the source of creation within each individual. In this sense, the spirit warrior's journey is akin to a sacred game, the moves of which require quick-witted improvisation and the purpose of which recedes ever further into the mists of sublime truth. This is a time for acting without calculation or premeditation. Trust that you have attained that elegance and ease of spirit which marks those whose self-confidence stems from a sense of inner preparedness that no external event can disturb. Find enjoyment in discovery and fulfillment in exploration, nurturing your curiosity with wonder and your playfulness with light-heartedness. Above all, don't dam up the source by fearing to make mistakes. If you rely on your intuition, instinct, and intention, then making ongoing adjustments and continuous corrections becomes the living path by which balance and harmony are achieved.

INTENT | Just as someone who has mastered a musical instrument can improvise at will, you are able to move through this time with an untroubled spirit, adapting and responding to sudden and unforeseen changes by initiating sudden and unforeseen changes of your own. Just as living music gains vitality and power when played by more than one musician, your efforts are in harmony with the unseen forces and aided by innumerable spirit helpers. Just as master musicians become the music they play, you become the moving source of renewal that you express. Just as the perennial presence of music is given new forms of expression every generation, your actions advance the collective work of renewing the perennial truth every generation.

SUMMARY | Reflect on those times in the past when you got stuck in opinions and a particular point of view. Think back on how exciting it was to break free of that oppression. Turn your attention to your present views and actions, identifying those which are damming up your joy of life and sense of discovery. Think forward to how exciting it will be to break free of that oppression.

THE LINE CHANGES

1ST   Meetings with something new are often clouded by emotions. First impressions, insights, and explanations are almost always more intuitive than comprehensive. Revisit those moments you encountered something for the first time and remove any definitions or decisions you formed then.

2ND   Not all partnerships last forever—one must end that the next may begin. But this need not be troubling—if companions know the road forks eventually, they part with the best of feelings when the time comes. Sudden as lightning, everything changes at once—you are in accord with fate.

3RD   Your peers take the road of speaking but you take the road of listening. Upon first hearing the message, they begin propagating it—you continue listening for its echoes in the relationships between things. The source of the river is high in the mountains and nearly uninhabited.

4TH   Having to publicly act on your ethics is difficult, especially when it comes at the expense of partnerships you value greatly. But parting ways when those you admire take the wrong road is a necessary step in the forging of your true self. Use this conflict to restore a wider unity.

5TH   Now you are ready to speak and your peers ready to listen. Their endeavors suddenly become tributaries of your endeavor's river. Once again, they rush to propagate the new message—and once again, you stay back, listening to the perennial murmur of the river's source.

6TH   You cannot control how others see you—but you can control how they don't see you. If you act like the stereotype people expect, it is your own fault for stepping off the path of freedom. Follow no example, mimic no one—leave a hole in the world when you are gone.

STAYING
OPEN

IMAGE | An infant beholds the many diverse items in its surroundings, each of which is calling to the child. The speech glyphs representing each article's voice are of different colors to show that the child's natural curiosity leads it to be fascinated by a wide array of interests.

INTERPRETATION | This hexagram depicts the openness of heart and mind and spirit of those who are adapting to the future. The infant symbolizes the living potential dwelling within every individual. The diverse objects around the child represent all the possible paths, both external and internal, lying before every individual at every turn. That the infant's attention is drawn to each of the interests means that you look at everything as an opportunity to develop yourself further. Taken together, these symbols mean that you are not adapted to one particular environment but, rather, to any environment.

ACTION | Spirit warriors do not lose heart when they realize they do not fit with their present surroundings. Instead, they maintain their training and discipline by exploring a wider range of interests and cultivating a wider variety of skills. This is an especially bad time to tolerate feelings of disappointment, lethargy, or self-pity. It is essential to keep in mind that the problem is simply the absence of meaningful opportunities facing you. Times change, inevitably bringing with them new opportunities. This is a time to prepare for the coming change by working to be adapted beforehand to the new environment. Because you are above all else adapted to learning and observation, you are in truth at home in any surroundings. But being able to survive is not as good as thriving—and even thriving is not as good as being able to contribute to the lives of others. By utilizing this time to build on your innate potential to learn and observe, you develop the knowledge and skills that enable you to take advantage of coming opportunities in a way that brings *benefit* to all in your surroundings. Avoid specializing in one area at this time. Because many of our capabilities are unknown to us until the opportunity to develop them presents itself, this is the time to energetically train for unknown opportunities rather than to resignedly commit to a meaningless and unfulfilling way of life.

INTENT | The ideal society is just like the ideal family, existing to afford every member the opportunity to develop their full potential. In times of darkness, however, authoritarianism restricts the creation of new opportunities and channels people into meaningless activities that benefit only those in authority. Societies change just like families do, transforming their goals and relationships with the passing of each generation. Whereas those who thrive in times of darkness cannot conceive a time of light, those who thrive in times of light can all too readily envision a return to darkness. Whether it is the individual, family, society, or humanity as a whole, the cycles of the pendulum's swings between the closing down and opening up of meaningful opportunities establishes the fundamental circumstances against which all actions take place and all decisions are made. The best way to contribute to the lives of others is to nurture and encourage their efforts to further develop their own potential. In this way, you materially assist others and help transform the fundamental circumstances within which all live.

SUMMARY | Cultivate as wide a range of interests and relationships as possible. Avoid the tendency to focus on one specific thing or person at this time. Cultivate breadth, not depth. It is a time of exploration, so follow your curiosity. Do not jump at the first opportunity or commit yourself to a single course of action now. Keep all your options open while you prepare for future opportunities.

THE LINE CHANGES

1ST Arrogance and gratitude are antithetical—but humility and gratitude go hand in hand. Only those who sense the existence of something greater than themselves are humble and grateful. Continue to devote yourself to something more than the materialistic pursuit of success and recognition.

2ND False modesty is more arrogant than outright arrogance—mere pretense is not equal to actually mastering the animal drives and emotions. A big fish in a little pond should not eat everything else in the pond. Cultivate authentic humility by pouring out sincere gratitude with every heartbeat.

3RD Believe in those around you, support their efforts, and encourage them when times are trying. When they see how this attitude results in your own accomplishments, their confidence will be renewed and they will redouble their efforts. Use your strengths to bolster others from below.

4TH To be subservient to someone with less skills, intelligence, or experience is more than most people can endure with grace and poise. Yet these circumstances are so common that no one should be unnerved by them any more. Hold the moral high ground and graciously serve your ideals.

5TH When those dependent on you interpret your humility as weakness, then they will be emboldened to criticize and undermine your efforts. You may try to correct them but it will not take, since they cannot lose face with their peers. The sooner and more decisively you root them out, the better.

6TH When those outside interpret your humility as weakness, then they will be emboldened to increase themselves at your expense. You should have already anticipated this inevitability. Now, use your yielding demeanor to draw the opponent into overreaching and then spring the trap.

NARROWING
AIM

IMAGE | A male warrior makes arrowheads by chipping them from a larger piece of obsidian. Finished arrowheads lie on the ground around him and an unfinished one falls away from the larger stone he has just struck. He strikes the larger stone with confidence and certainty, each action's precision the result of long and diligent practice.

INTERPRETATION | This hexagram depicts those who narrow their focus. The male warrior symbolizes the training and discipline that increases an individual's versatility and fortitude. That he makes arrowheads by chipping them from a larger piece of stone means that you succeed by narrowing your larger vision down to definable and achievable goals. The finished arrowheads symbolize the experience, learning, and skill you have already acquired. The unfinished arrowhead falling away from the block of obsidian symbolizes your present endeavor, which comes out well because you can rely on the strengths you have developed through past efforts. That great practice has made him confident and effective means that your actions achieve their desired effects because you never stop perfecting your craft. Taken together, these symbols mean that you bring *benefit* to others by narrowing the totality of your interests down to the specific purpose at hand.

ACTION | The masculine half of the spirit warrior serves the whole by mastering the part. Grand schemes and long-range plans come to pass only through the slow accumulation of well-aimed actions and timely responses: This is not the time for great visions but, rather, for small and perfectly executed deeds. Even the smallest of our successes and the greatest of our failures contribute to our mastering that aspect of life we are called to specialize in: This is not the time for regrets or dreams but, rather, for practical and immediate results. Experience is built up over a long period of time and not just mastered overnight: This is not the time for impatience or arrogance but, rather, for devoting ourselves to a lifetime apprenticeship of practice and learning. Creativity without results is sterile, understanding without acts is self-indulgent: This is not the time for beginning new wide-ranging projects but, rather, for completing narrowly focused goals already initiated. Through long repetition and genuine sincerity, practice is transformed into mastery and mastery into service: This is not the time for self-satisfaction or self-importance but, rather, for placing our endeavor in the service of that which is greater than ourselves.

INTENT | When your true aim is to manifest the spirit you have always believed yourself to be, your every action, no matter how seemingly insignificant, hits the target. There are innumerable excuses for not making spiritual progress but they all boil down to a failure to act as we know we should. Only by ignoring distractions and eliminating compulsiveness can we stop being dragged around by our attention and begin to direct it toward the purpose of real moment. Actors may take on different roles and act in many different ways but beneath all those various external appearances they sustain the true intent to prove themselves the quality of actor they have always believed themselves to be. It is in this sense that we must not lose ourselves in the roles and actions of everyday life but, rather, comport ourselves with the dignity and wisdom and generosity of a noble and powerful spirit. In this way we narrow the uncountable aims of the body down to the spirit warrior's single aim of contributing materially to the well-being of the whole.

SUMMARY | You have spread yourself too thin trying to accomplish too many things at once. It is essential that you decide upon the order in which things need to be done and then complete each in turn. Moving back and forth between different activities is not allowing you to develop your skills or vision or relationships as you should. Finish what you have started before starting over.

THE LINE CHANGES

1ST   What you take for granted is changing, leading to momentous surprises. While the self does not age, the body does—and the emotions are always trying to catch up with changes the body has already undergone. Use each stage of life to remind yourself that you are not your body.

2ND   Your strength of personality can overshadow those around you—know when to step aside and let others shine. You learn more about yourself by not doing what comes easily than by falling into predictable routines. Treat your loved ones as great mysteries and they will astonish you.

3RD   A new opportunity presents itself, one that promises rapid advancement and certain profit. What you do now reveals much about your character to you—do you fulfill your duty or do you pursue a mirage? Choose loyalty over cleverness and persistence over sudden gain.

4TH   Follow your curiosity and it evolves into a hobby which evolves, in turn, into a passion and thence into expertise. Your love of learning new things leads you to participate on a deeper level with the people and nature around you. Be interested in anything but yourself.

5TH   The window of opportunity opens—people both above and below respond favorably to you and offer their support. Incorporate their interests and goals into your own, letting them lead for the time being. Incorporate their thinking into your own, letting them prepare you to take the lead later.

6TH   Your life purpose hangs, like the pre-dawn sun, just below the horizon of your vision—all it needs to rise is a welcoming invitation. Turn your attention away from trivialities and toward a dream you had forgotten until now. Abandon the outer distractions in favor of a single-minded remembering.

LIVING
ESSENCE

IMAGE | An acorn hangs from a twig, a great oak tree already fully grown within it. The noonday sun shines in the cloudless sky above.

INTERPRETATION | This hexagram depicts the spirit of the seed, which contains all of creation within its secret heart. The acorn symbolizes the living potential that dwells within every individual creation. The tree already grown within the seed symbolizes the fulfilled promise of potential that is already alive within every creation. The trunk of that tree symbolizes the long continuity of your spiritual lineage, its branches symbolize the sheltering and protection of your spirit, and its roots symbolize your hidden foundation. The twig from which the acorn hangs is a symbol of the preceding generations, which continue to live and create. The noonday sun in a cloudless sky symbolizes the full force of divine love, which creates and sustains all of creation. Taken together, these symbols mean that you accept your blessings with the sole intent of returning them tenfold to the world.

ACTION | The spirit warrior wins the sacred war against the enemy-within by keeping what is alive and shedding what is dead. For the spirit warrior, that which is alive is the essential and indestructible purity of the soul. Where the enemy-within seeks to keep alive all the impurities that defeat the soul's best intentions, the spirit warrior sheds each impurity as soon as it is discovered. By living wholly in the purity of the seed, the spirit warrior allows each dead leaf to fall away as soon as its season passes. It is a time for filling your heart with the depth of compassion that inspires genuine acts of benevolence and loving-kindness. The power to bring *benefit* to others obeys the same law as water: The channel which is most empty and clear of obstructions carries the greatest abundance. Because you are motivated by selfless compassion rather than a desire for personal evolution or achievement, you are carried along by the very *benefit* you bring to others. From tree to seed and from seed to tree, the living essence of *benefit* passes. Concentrate on the *need* of others and you find this the most creative and rewarding of times, clear away all inner obstructions and you convey *benefit* directly from the source.

Because you keep the living seed of loving-kindness alive, you shed the dead leaves of self-interest without even trying. Of all the roads home, the road of simplicity has the least obstructions.

INTENT | Essence recognizes essence: Voice and echo belong to one another, face and reflection are not different. Shedding the differences between things, the spirit warrior keeps alive that which makes them the same—because all things share a common origin, they share a common destiny. Happiness, well-being, success, and love all flow from the same source—that from which all partake and none may be excluded. Just as the sun shines on all equally, the living potential of spirit is as strong in all as it is in one—and, just as darkness reigns until the sun first rises, we do not awaken this living essence until we keep the gate of the untroubled spirit open and the gate of the troubled spirit closed. By cultivating an untroubled spirit, we are able to see through the world of appearances and into the world of essence within which we already live.

SUMMARY | Just because you can do something doesn't mean you should: Know what to turn down. Simplify your life. Don't waste your energy. Avoid excitement and exaggeration. Be patient and kind. Slow down. Stop thinking about your own feelings and needs. Try to benefit others, especially the future generations. This is the most productive time of your life—what will you make?

THE LINE CHANGES

1ST   Too much idle conjecturing about matters that have not yet occurred results in physical and emotional distress. Take your mind off purposeless imaginings by engaging in physical activities. Make no plans, decisions, or commitments now.

2ND   Your vision resonates with others, bringing you lifelong allies. Document your emerging vision since you will want to revisit it later. Consider the words of your predecessors before deciding on a long-range goal.

3RD   Even those able to use their creative vision to make a living often find this diminishes their creativity. It is best to keep the two separate, at least for the time being. Work, explore, investigate—the landscape is filled with vast tracts of untrod terrain.

4TH   If your vision serves others, then it is time to make it public. If it still serves its own unfolding, then it is still time to keep it private. If in doubt, it is best to work in private—you may be tempted to share your ideas with those close to you but avoid doing so until your vision has crystallized.

5TH   The window of opportunity opens—you enter the height of creative power, your ability to give your vision expression reaches its peak. Do not hesitate to extend your influence as far as possible. Look for ways to reach people that others have not imagined.

6TH   When the imaginative power wanes, stop producing new work. Return to the origins of your vision and rework them in light of what you know now. Do not listen to others appealing to your vanity for their own self-interest.

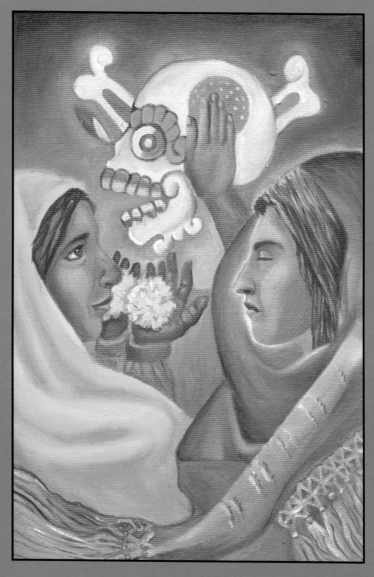

GROWING
CERTAINTY

IMAGE | Two female warriors confront death. One closes her eyes and holds up her hand in a gesture of rejection and denial. The other looks upon death like an old friend, holding out flowers in a gesture of both offering and accepting.

INTERPRETATION | This hexagram depicts a blossoming of convictions. The two female warriors symbolize opposing views of what is real and true. The skeletal figure of death symbolizes the inevitability of change and transformation. The warrior who closes her eyes and rejects death symbolizes fear of the unknown. The warrior who holds out flowers and accepts death symbolizes trust in the world beyond the senses. The flowers she offers symbolize the perfection of the world as it is. Taken together, these symbols mean that your convictions continue to evolve in a time of burgeoning social, political, and religious movements.

ACTION | The feminine half of the spirit warrior does not step off the path of wisdom. Times of change bring with them the desire for permanent values and rules of behavior, creating conflicts between those who wish to institutionalize the new changes and those who wish to enforce the old. If we take our eyes off the perennial and become absorbed with the ephemeral, then we are caught in the sway of history's pendulum as it swings between its predictable extremes of action and backlash, action and backlash—yet if we do not respond to the genuine *need* of others, then we lack both compassion and courage. Similarly, if we allow ourselves to be swept up in the passions of others' convictions, then we face the predictable betrayal of values and purpose that every institution, cause, and movement commits—yet if we do not contribute to the world in a meaningful way, then we betray our own values and purpose. In this sense, the path of wisdom is that place where the path of compassion and the path of freedom intersect: Neither governed by others' ideas of right and wrong nor hiding behind a wall of selfishness and cynicism, we allow our understanding to evolve and grow while we consistently perform good works. It is a time for remaining secure in your belief that the truth continues to unfold as you continue to explore the great mystery that is life.

INTENT | Those who are convinced of their rightness commit many wrongs, those who seek revenge cause themselves great suffering. Only by observing the long-range effects of self-righteousness can we stop perpetuating the cycle of action and backlash, action and backlash. True certainty revolves around the inevitable transformation of all things, the quintessential symbol of which is physical death. Because this inevitable confrontation with the unknown is shared by all living beings, it forms a bond of understanding and compassion that holds all life sacred—and, because recognizing our own fear of the unknown allows us to appreciate the suffering it causes in others, we have within our individual experience the foundation upon which to build our collective monument to the sacredness of all life. Because you accept the passing away of all ephemeral perfection with a loving and trusting heart, your contribution—your offering—to the undying perfection of the world is accepted by the spirit of metamorphosis. Cultivate inner courage and outer compassion and you transmute sterile certainty into an ever-unfolding blossom of loving wisdom.

SUMMARY | Commit yourself to acting on the truth wholeheartedly—but remember that your understanding and interpretation of the truth is evolving and unfolding as always. Avoid surrounding yourself with others who think like you, seek out different points of view. Do not allow your convictions to be set in mental stone—you want them to be living, growing, ever-ripening fruits of your heart.

THE LINE CHANGES

1ST When people break out into the open and put dreariness behind them, they are understandably enthusiastic and often overconfident. It suddenly seems possible to accomplish anything and they reach for the moon. Everything is moving in a wonderful direction—as long as you go slow.

2ND The window of opportunity opens—it seems like the shutters are taken down and golden sunlight fills the world after the dark storm passes. Don't keep to yourself—let your joy overflow into the lives of your loved ones. Strengthen your bonds with those accompanying you to the end.

3RD A big part of your life comes to an end—will you celebrate or grieve? Transitions are a natural part of life, the way endings are knotted back into new beginnings—the way the cycle of creation renews itself. Let go the past, be grateful for all you've learned, and lean forward into the oncoming wind.

4TH When people are rude, insolent, and offensive it is because they do not believe there is any real consequence to their actions. Such persons cause disturbance everywhere they go—starting out bad, they just get worse. Let them go quickly and without a second thought.

5TH When people who are fortunate complain and bemoan their lot in life, it is because they have lost touch with humanity and can no longer hear how they sound. Such persons will not help you—it is best to go your own way. They won't accept your help, either—they have powerful friends above.

6TH In order to protect what is valuable and sustain this period of peace as long as possible, it is necessary to confront an openly hostile faction. Disprove its accusations and prove its wrongdoings—isolate its leadership and win over its followers. Do not allow this problem to fester.

MASTERING
REASON

IMAGE | A male warrior kneels beside a stone marker counting off the thirteen steps leading to the top of a pyramid. Atop the pyramid, an ancient spirit, part female and part male, squats before the ceremonial drum and balances the forces of water and fire. The warrior's face is raised to gaze with wonder and reverence upon the spirit of duality above.

INTERPRETATION | This hexagram depicts reason humbling itself before the transcendental. The male warrior symbolizes the masculine creative force, who tests and trains human nature in order to increase its versatility and fortitude. The pyramid symbolizes human works that mirror the sacred mountain standing forever at the center of the world. The thirteen steps of the pyramid symbolize the single set of laws that govern both the realm of matter and the realm of spirit. The ancient spirit that is part male and part female symbolizes the absolute unity of the duality of creation. The forces of fire and water that the ancient spirit balances symbolize the act of creation whereby everything is formed of two complementary halves. The ceremonial drum symbolizes human action following the eternal rhythm of the heartbeat of all creation. That the warrior's face is upraised in wonder and reverence means that reason is not an end in itself but, rather, must serve something higher than itself. Taken together, these symbols mean that you complement the logic of reason with the love of creation.

ACTION | The masculine half of the spirit warrior advances toward the spiritual logic of the first ancestor. This a time for reining in the authority of the intellect in order to achieve greater balance and harmony in your life. Not until we accept that many of our beliefs are either opinions we have received from others or conclusions we have leapt to based on insufficient experience do we allow our thoughts to follow their natural line of reasoning. Once we accept that matter is spirit and that nature is the sacred, then we no longer allow our intellect to pursue avenues that deaden the human spirit, dehumanize society, and desecrate nature. We cultivate instead a higher form of reason that is tempered by its other half. Opening our heart to the sacredness of everything in creation, true reason becomes a path by which we approach ever closer our destination in the divine intelligence of the creative forces. Because you hold everything in the visible world sacred, you are blessed by the unseen forces. Because you train your mind to follow the path of spiritual cause-and-effect, you are blessed in the visible world.

INTENT | When the heart understands, the mind feels. Only when our heart perceives the world as it truly is does our mind have a foundation upon which to build. Without an abiding love for all creation, our mind is set adrift on the sea of fear, doubt, and endless speculation. Without a heartfelt understanding of human nature, our thinking is cold, calculating, and devoid of conscience. By observing the laws governing the way things interact and develop in the realm of nature, we grasp the laws governing the way things interact and develop in the realm of spirit. By rigorously training our mind to see in the visible a clear vision of the invisible, our mind becomes a mirror of the laws governing nature and spirit.

SUMMARY | You cannot solve your problems by reason alone, since it is reason that tells you why things cannot be solved. You must really place yourself in the hands of spirit now and trust in the power and love of something greater than yourself. Visualize yourself happy and well and speak to spirit in those images and pictures. Stop the rationalizing mind. See everything as sacred, including yourself.

THE LINE CHANGES

1ST Be concerned with the physical and emotional stress that has been endured for a while. It is a time to slow your pace and not place undue demands on others or yourself. Listen to your body and heart—rest and relax and catch your breath before going on.

2ND People find themselves estranged, having concentrated so forcefully on their goal that the partnership has been taken for granted. It is a time to break through all the little barriers between you. Be light-hearted and all your closeness and intimacy will return.

3RD Be concerned with old disagreements that threaten to erupt anew and disrupt the existing equilibrium. It is not that you are not strong enough to win—it is the harm that conflict would inflict on the new venture. Be strong enough to win by maintaining peace.

4TH People find themselves uneasy, unsure of what misfortune might strike out of nowhere. While it is wise to be wary, it is foolish to be timid—you have the resources to stave off any counterattacks. Practice the art of renewal, don't become part of the old.

5TH Be concerned with the manner in which you conduct yourself and the message it conveys. Successful leadership is neither arrogant nor indecisive—it is confidently responsive to circumstances. Exude sincere good will and you will gain the trust of all.

6TH People find themselves alone and alienated, surprised they have driven off the very allies they sought to defend. Sense this now, before it is too late—you depend on others more than you realize. Dispense loving-kindness instead of ideas and all ends well.

REPEATING
TEST

IMAGE | A male warrior wearing the emblem of the smoking mirror pauses in his tracks. The true road runs straight ahead but the warrior's footprints show that he has doubled back on himself, circling around a pool of water. The day sky overhead is filled with sunlight but the pool reflects the full moon in the night sky, indicating that the warrior made that past part of his journey in the dark of night. As he prepares to undertake this leg of his journey for the second time, the warrior must face the additional danger of a jaguar who now crouches beside the pool.

INTERPRETATION | This hexagram depicts someone facing a dilemma for the second time. The male warrior symbolizes the challenges and self-discipline that make us stronger and more adaptable than we imagined. The smoking mirror symbolizes the penetrating insight, introspection, and self-knowledge required if we are to achieve a vision of the true self. That he pauses in his tracks means that you take the opportunity to slow down your decisions in order to consider your circumstances carefully and discern how they resemble a past experience you have long wished to rectify. That he has stepped off the true road to circle around the pool means that your true destiny must wait while you return to a previous stage in order to complete its task. That it is light now but the pool reflects the night sky means that you are more aware and capable now than you were when you first encountered this test. That this part of the journey is complicated by the additional danger of a jaguar lying in wait means that you clearly perceive this to be a new situation even as you use it to change your spiritual history. Taken together, these symbols mean that you heal wounds left from a past stage of development.

ACTION | The masculine half of the spirit warrior gazes into the smoking mirror of the true self without blinking. It is a time for exhibiting the character traits you believe you should have exhibited when facing a similar dilemma in the past. Because you take advantage of this second chance to prove yourself to yourself, you erase past regrets and reveal your true self to the unseen forces. By turning our perception upon ourselves, we are able to sense the lessons we have learned from past mistakes. Until we have had the opportunity to act on those lessons and put them into effect, however, part of us remains frozen at that stage of our development. For that reason, there are few more fortuitous times than those in which we can prove we are stronger and wiser than in the past. By discerning our own patterns of behavior that run consistently beneath the surface of appearances, we are able to stop repeating past mistakes and emerge victorious over our own self-defeating attitudes and behaviors. Because you intuitively know that turning points periodically return until they are finally resolved, you are fully prepared to act when the time comes. Because you wait vigilantly for the opportunity to revisit a period of darkness, you do not fail to use the present turning point to extend the continuity of your light further back into the past.

INTENT | Now is the time to strengthen the ladder of your evolution by descending it in order to repair a lower rung. Actions and decisions that have haunted us must be laid to rest if we are to advance further toward our rightful destiny. Within the inner landscape of our soul there are hurdles we failed to clear, pitfalls we failed to avoid, on our first encounter—where we first reacted with weakness we can now react with strength, where we first acted naively we can now act wisely, where we first reacted with fear we can now react with confidence, where we first acted selfishly we can now act lovingly. Because you do not allow this opportunity to correct the past to slip through your hands, you break the chains holding you and your allies back from ascending to the next rung of success.

SUMMARY | Don't make the same mistake again. Some fears are false fears, some hopes are false hopes: Stop and consider how you are reverting to a way of thinking, feeling, and acting that did not work before. You are stronger and wiser now—act as you wish you had acted the first time. Seize this opportunity to heal the past and you will create the future you long for.

THE LINE CHANGES

1ST   Many are in denial of the growing trend toward oppression—all you can do is join with those of like mind and prepare for what lies ahead. Avoid controversial positions and don't call attention to your efforts. Make yourselves useful but anonymous.

2ND   Many cannot avoid the first trap—all you can do is appreciate the cunning of those above and go along with it for now. There will be time to fight for principles later but the priority now must be just surviving this time. Do not provoke envy or resentment by flaunting your little success.

3RD   Only the high-minded can avoid the second trap—do not even make an attempt to adapt to this situation. Withdraw into what seclusion you can muster and rely on your companions to see you through. To participate in this corruption would cause lifelong regret.

4TH   The darkness itself begins to wane as even some of its adherents start to question their own actions. Your integrity and practicality draw some of these people to you. Remain extremely cautious and do not take unwarranted risks, but these relationships hold potential for wresting order from chaos.

5TH   The situation is auspicious—you are at the vanguard of sweeping changes that will benefit all but those you replace. The principal task for now is to brighten the emotional atmosphere and give everyone hope. Slow down—actually implementing the new will take a long time.

6TH   The dam breaks—the last vestiges of oppression dissolve, the will of its leadership is broken, and the waters of free-thinking and creativity rush forward again. Celebrate with those around you. Spend your time training the next generation, for without continuity of principles it will all happen again.

INTERNALIZING
PURITY

IMAGE | At the base of a pyramid, a male warrior records the oral tradition passed on to him by a female warrior. As he paints the teachings in a screen-fold manuscript, the spirit of the tradition becomes a living presence within him.

INTERPRETATION | Where a pyramid symbolizes human creations that stand against time like nature's own mountains, the pyramid's base is a symbol of that part which is absolutely the last to be eroded away. The male warrior symbolizes the training and self-discipline required to subdue self-defeating attitudes and behavior. The oral tradition, represented by a blue speech glyph, symbolizes the living memory of a way of life that is in balance and in harmony with nature and spirit. The female warrior symbolizes the nourishing and compassion required to inspire dignity and benevolence. Just as a footprint in the sand is not the living person who passed along the shore, the teachings painted in the manuscript symbolize a static and limited view of a living way of life. The spirit of the tradition becoming a living presence within him symbolizes the permanent transformation of human nature required to live in balance and in harmony with nature and spirit. Taken together, these symbols mean that you fill your spirit so full of the living vision of light and liberty and loving-kindness that no opposing thought may enter.

ACTION | The masculine half of the spirit warrior upholds the feminine half of the spirit warrior within. In times when power is abused and the human spirit oppressed, it is essential to stand against the tide of corruption without getting corrupted. This requires an integration of wisdom and courage that provides resistance to an artificial way of life without being corrupted by contact with it. Only when we are inspired by a vision of the inherent purity and perfection of human nature can we live in the sphere of aggression and exploitation without being contaminated by the greed, ambition, anger, and fear it propagates. Likewise, it is only when we are inspired to revere all of nature and spirit that we can live in the sphere of destruction and desecration without being infected by the materialism and narcissism it propagates. Because you have the self-discipline to purify yourself of self-defeating attitudes and behavior, you are like a great boulder of gold that a stream of filth can neither taint nor move. Because you have the heartfelt openness to love and nourish all things equally, you are like a bottomless well of spring water that can neither be fouled nor exhausted. Bring the vision of a balanced and harmonious way of life into your heart, inscribe the vision of a pure face and a pure heart into the stone of your spirit, make the vision of light and liberty and loving-kindness into the pyramid of your lifework. This living purity you so adore in others and in nature is also within you—allow yourself to adore this spark of the divine within yourself and you are like a nurse in the midst of a plague, tending to the stricken without falling ill yourself.

INTENT | Even as others create a sphere of darkness, we create a sphere of light. Consider the *need* of both those who manufacture an artificial way of life and those who accept it as their own way of life: Whether it is the former's desire to control others or the latter's desire to live in a controlled world, both suffer from a profound distrust of nature, humanity, and spirit. Observe the crippling effects of this *need* when it goes unchecked and unremedied. Attend to what the powerful are willing to take and what the powerless are willing to give up. Look at the world of darkness and despair they create out of this tragic *need*. Take refuge in the ancient way of life: Establish balance and harmony with nature and spirit, form alliances with people of like mind, let your heart overflow with the *benefit* of trust in all creation. Bring the light of purity into your heart and you are brought into the sphere of the purity of light.

SUMMARY | You are in too much of a hurry. You want to take action and get matters resolved quickly, becoming frustrated and overly critical when things do not move at your pace. Where a stranger sees only an infant, a father sees a noble warrior. Where a layperson sees only rough glass, a diamond cutter sees a priceless jewel. Become blind to the impurities for now, see only the purity before you.

The Line Changes

1ST   A perceived threat is not the same as a real threat—you are in no danger unless you actually treat this as real and react in some way to it. Don't get unnerved and try to solve a problem that does not exist. You've done this before—step back and smile at your excitability.

2ND   At a certain point, problems are only made worse by talking about them further—to save this partnership, quit opening the wound and let it heal. Use your anger and hurt to fuel your external undertakings. Hold firm to your dignity and long-range goals and this rift between you will close.

3RD   There are cycles of centralizing authority for increased control and decentralizing it for increased innovation—the transitions between these cycles are especially difficult to adjust to. Quit caring so much, this isn't personal—you are too invested in this. Put your attention back on your home life.

4TH   There are those whose attitudes have contributed significantly to your exhaustion—now, as you move away from the past, is the time to let those relationships go all at once. This change offers a good rationale for breaking away. To continue these associations would demean you.

5TH   Sometimes it is an internal change, not an external one, that triggers disengagement—leaving what the heart no longer desires in order to engage in something higher holds great promise. Even at the height of success, stepping back onto the road of freedom cannot be wrong. Few will understand.

6TH   Absolute disengagement, as a way of life, frees you from the attachments and entanglements that so confound most people. Paradoxically, it allows you to be more engaged with life by freeing you from the desire to control the consequences of your actions. You live in a sea of circulating benefit.

RECAPTURING
VISION

IMAGE | Descending from the sun, a hummingbird impregnates a female warrior whose posture and gesture signify that she actively invites the creative forces to bring forth a new creation through her.

INTERPRETATION | This hexagram depicts reawakened idealism. The hummingbird descending from the sun symbolizes the spirits of great warriors who return from the house of the sun to inspire the living. The female warrior is symbolic of one trusting life and serving spirit in order to bring *benefit* to all. That she actively invites the creative forces to bring forth a new creation through her means that you possess the openness of spirit and the joy of life to conceive and nurture an endeavor that reflects the underlying perfection of the world. Taken together, these symbols mean that your every act is a sincere effort to bring the external world into accord with the original dream of spirit.

ACTION | The feminine half of the spirit warrior is fulfilled by the will to create. We enter this world with memories of those principles which should govern personal and social conduct—principles that call us to task, demanding that we seek the good and the beautiful, demanding that we honor and respect all life, demanding that we have the opportunity to fulfill our full potential, demanding that we live compassionately and joyfully. Yet our memories of these principles grow dim over time as we are exposed to the cruelty and suffering pervading the world—and dimmer still as we seek to establish a secure and stable life while surrounded by so many others competing for a similar goal. In times of darkness the sun seems very far away, yet its light and warmth are here among us every day. Although senseless suffering and mad cruelty seem to govern people's lives everywhere, the loving guidance of the unseen ancestors is present among us every moment. Because you actively invite spirit to make use of you to bring its principles to life, you recapture the vision with which you came into the world and rededicate yourself to its fulfillment. It is not a time to hold back for fear of being impractical or naive, since your sincerity, passion, and integrity make it possible to achieve real and lasting changes. Nor is it a time to hold back for fear of losing to superior forces, since your hope, compassion, and courage eventually win over opponents to your endeavor. Radiate unfading optimism and unqualified love for people everywhere and your efforts inspire others to risk sharing your vision. Demonstrate principled action and steadfast devotion to the divine spark in every life and you make yourself a worthy vehicle for the creative forces.

INTENT | Personal success is secondary to bringing *benefit* to others, personal longings are secondary to the legitimate *need* of others. All people deserve the same rights, all cultures are created equal. We benefit from the efforts of our ancestors, our descendants must benefit from our efforts. We benefit from what our environment produces; our environment must benefit from what we produce. We share a common origin with all life, we share a common destiny with all spirit. Principles must reflect the underlying harmony of the world, ideals must be put into action.

SUMMARY | You are procrastinating. Your conscience demands things be acted on and the hour is growing late. Don't find excuses to keep you from speaking and acting as you should. Now is the time to channel your righteous indignation into creative acts that touch others' hearts. Rage not against injustices done to you, but against the injustices done to others. The momentum is with you.

THE LINE CHANGES

1ST Strong-willed and independent, you do not let those above influence your lifestyle. This is all well and good—but you must exercise the same independence from the opinions of those you count as peers. Avoid fads and fashions—let the inner determine the outer, not the other way around.

2ND Relationships are not like jewelry, meant to impress others and improve one's social standing. The fact that others act precisely in this manner makes your own conduct all that much more important. How and why you choose the friends and partners you do is a most telling aspect of your character.

3RD Lax ethics everywhere abound—it can be sorely tempting to go along with those who appear to be benefiting from impropriety. Making a past that has to be covered up, however, is not the way to improve your standard of living now. Promote yourself without lowering yourself.

4TH You feel you are too good to settle for either of the choices before you, yet you are too impatient to wait for another opportunity. This is thinking too much about appearances and not enough about the inner worth of all concerned. No matter what you decide, your attitude must mature.

5TH Success has not spoiled you—you set a standard for refined simplicity and effectiveness that your peers criticize and refuse to emulate. Because you are attuned to the time, however, you are soon vindicated. Make every facet of your life consistent with your principles.

6TH No longer concerned with appearances at all, your lifestyle reflects your concern for comfort and functionality. You have come to adorn yourself as nature adorns itself—clouds in the sky, lakes on the land, snow on the mountains, jewels underground. Continue refining your inner gold.

DEFYING
UNCERTAINTY

IMAGE | A female warrior stands in the middle of a great waterfall, holding a lighted torch in a way that protects it from going out. She stands naked in the wilderness, surrounded only by tall mountains and deep valleys, far from the security of home and loved ones. The waterfall's current takes on the form of continuous speech glyphs in order to show the deafening and unceasing roar of the cascade.

INTERPRETATION | This hexagram depicts the power of not being swept away by the times. The waterfall symbolizes the uncontrollable momentum of events to which you stand exposed. The torch symbolizes how your attitude and actions affect others. The female warrior symbolizes the sensitivity and loving-kindness that is at the core of inner strength. That she keeps the torch from being extinguished by the torrent of water means that you dwell in a sphere of peace and equilibrium even as crisis and uncertainty rage around you. That she stands naked and alone in the wilderness means that you are unafraid to stand exposed to the elements of change. The deafening and unceasing roar of the cascade symbolizes the universal hymn of change, turbulence, and the unforeseen. Taken together, these symbols mean that you keep the flame of spirit alive by eradicating every self-defeating thought and fearful emotion before they have time to take root.

ACTION | The feminine half of the spirit warrior does not lose faith in the path. Gold must pass through fire before it is pure, the heart must pass through doubt before it is true: Just as gold allows itself to be refined by fire, the heart must allow itself to be tested by doubt. When our circumstances are difficult and distressing and impossible to control, then there is only one thing we can control—how we react to our circumstances. When we face an unknown and unpredictable future, then there is only one thing we can know—how we are treating the present. This is neither the time to worry about what might happen nor the time to ruminate on what might have been: Put all your past lessons and self-discipline into practice now, sensing your peace of mind and feeling your reverence for the living moment. Let the current of change pass through you and around you and past you and, in the end, only your strong, wise, and loving nature remains. Because you react to troubled times by maintaining an untroubled spirit, you continue to advance where others feel compelled to retreat. Because you trust and revere the present moment, the flame of your faith allows you to continue bringing *benefit* to your surroundings.

INTENT | The path of the spirit warrior does not lead to a final destination but, rather, to ever greater levels of understanding and responsibility. This perpetual journey takes us through some difficult terrain, demanding that our understandings be based on personal experience and our responsibilities be fulfilled with heartfelt compassion. Because we cannot bring *benefit* to another's *need* that we have not filled in ourselves, it is necessary to overcome every trial of faith ourselves. Here it is not the strong and unyielding nature of the masculine half of the spirit warrior who endures the ordeal but, rather, the nurturing and open-hearted nature of the feminine half. Now is the time to cultivate the inner strength that makes possible outer nurturing by conscientiously eliminating every thought, emotion, and memory that casts doubt on the majesty and grandeur of creation. Allow only your faith in something greater than yourself to flower in the garden of your soul and, inevitably, you emerge with the degree of understanding and power you need to fulfill the next stage of responsibility.

SUMMARY | Although you are close to the prize, things have become more complicated and more difficult than expected. You must embody the principle of resistance and stand against the crushing weight of fear, doubt, and worry longer than expected. Keep the flame of your dream alive and you will have much to celebrate— but let it go out and it will take a long time for you to regain your momentum.

THE LINE CHANGES

1ST Not taking warnings seriously, you are neither cautious nor attentive. The dangers are very real and easy to fall into—good advice always sounds like a cliché until the moment it proves true, at which point it's too late to take. Once again: This is like a tiger trap in the road—just step around it.

2ND Communication is blocked because you are echoing the same thing over and over. This is a time to ask yourself what you are not understanding rather than demand that the other understand better. Things don't have to be like this—be patient enough to seek one small improvement at a time.

3RD Indecisive one moment, arbitrary the next—this is not the way to acquire a good reputation. If you want to work alongside the best, you must respond to both the immediate and long-range conditions at the same time. Stop trying so hard for a while—watch others and learn from their actions.

4TH When your allies stumble they drag you into trouble with them. Thrashing about will not do any good now—maintain your composure and your dignity. There are others who support you and who will clear your name—in time, your actions will vindicate others' trust in you.

5TH The liabilities faced in this situation are daunting—you have done everything possible to prepare for the worst and yet that may not be enough. Now the dice must be thrown—do you go ahead or not? So much is riding on this—if you have doubts, losing face over a delay is the middle path.

6TH Can one have penetrating insight and be pessimistic—can one have wisdom and advocate despair? Superficial learning convinces people that the end is approaching—profound learning proves that renewal is always present. Pull your thoughts, emotions, words, and deeds back onto the path.

DAWNING
EXISTENCE

IMAGE | As the sun rises behind it, a flowering tree branches out into different kinds of animals.

INTERPRETATION | This hexagram depicts the spirit of the flower, which brings all the potential of creation to full bloom. The rising sun symbolizes the eternal renewal of the world. The tree branching out into different animals is a symbol of the multiplicity of forms making up the single body of creation. The tree's flowers symbolize the perfection of each passing moment of eternity. Taken together, these symbols mean that you successfully complete your task because you further the interests of those you serve.

ACTION | The spirit warrior wins the sacred war against the enemy-within by emulating the loving-kindness of land and water. Seeds of great trees may be brought forth in great number but they amount to nothing unless they fall upon fertile soil and receive proper watering. Similarly, seeds of great deeds may arise in great number but if such visions are not treated reverentially and nurtured carefully, then they eventually come to naught. It is for this reason that the spirit warrior receives every idea and inspiration and motive just as the land receives each seed and just as water nourishes every plant. Because no one can say which vision is destined to produce a great deed, every thought and feeling and action needs to be treated with the respect due a prodigy of incalculable potential. When land and water become our teachers, then we foster spirit everywhere we touch it. To be truly beneficial, however, our fostering has to be spontaneous, natural, and without self-interest. Following the model of earth and water, we bring seeds to completion without any contrived actions, conscious influence, or ulterior motives. This is a time for revisiting the issue of service and expanding your definition of whom you serve and how you best serve them. Because the *need* of those you serve has changed nearly as much as your own understanding, this is a propitious time to rededicate yourself to bringing *benefit* to others with ever-growing joy and devotion. You succeed because you strive for others' success: Because you open your heart and embrace all you touch, you are blessed with the resourcefulness to bring your task to successful completion.

INTENT | A heart that is accepting and caring is the sign of an untroubled spirit. Just as land and water love every seed equally, we must open our spirit to the whole of existence that is blossoming around us. Just as land and water are themselves seeds within the greater earth and sky, we must allow our spirit to be loved by the greater spirit of existence that is renewing itself everywhere at all times. You germinate, take root, grow, flower, and put forth your own seeds because you serve as land and water for others. Because you sense the flowering of perfection all around you, you are blessed with an understanding of your task that is renewing itself every lifetime and every generation.

SUMMARY | The tests are passed, you are entering a long period of success and contentment. The trials are over, you have the freedom to make a valuable contribution to the lives of others. Like a commoner one day appointed adviser to the king and queen, your concerns and demeanor change overnight. Even this time of fulfillment cannot last forever, though, so make it a time you can be proud of forever.

THE LINE CHANGES

1ST   Before taking up the other's work, make yourself strong and stable. Do not ignore the symptoms of physical or emotional distress that could worsen with time. Take care of yourself first so that your service to the higher will not be interrupted later.

2ND   Your bond with the other is unbreakable, forged as it is out of heartfelt devotion to a superior vision. Take up this cause with unadulterated enthusiasm and confidence, bringing the full weight of your experience and will to bear. Act with ease and spontaneity—you have found your path in life.

3RD   Investing your time and effort in this project will ultimately be rewarding even though nothing concrete will materialize soon. Work to increase the feasibility of the endeavor reaching many people and benefiting their lives. Do not lose faith in your partnership.

4TH   If you merely try to protect your own interests, the alliance will fall apart. If you feel you are being taken advantage of, or that serving others does not fulfill your own needs, then all your good efforts will be negated by resentment. Be genuinely grateful for this opportunity and things will improve.

5TH   Do not compete for recognition or status—yours is the power to bring matters to fruition, not the power to overwhelm. You are an essential part of an important undertaking—do not get confused or distracted by success. The seeds of future happiness are in the very fruit ripening before you.

6TH   You can go no further with this work without going back and taking up a serious study of the issues at hand. Stop working on this endeavor until you have absorbed a whole new program of learning. There may be new projects to undertake before returning to complete this one.

DEVELOPING
POTENTIAL

IMAGE | As the sun sets behind the mountains, a female warrior chants while she offers water to the four directions of the desert wilderness. The water she pours into the sand is drawn with jade beads and small conch shells. In the foreground of the scene a great maguey cactus grows.

INTERPRETATION | This hexagram depicts the spirit of seeds that still remain hidden. The four directions symbolize the full range of the spirit warrior's action, which encompasses both the sphere of the world and the circle of the seasons. The desert wilderness symbolizes the inner landscape of achievement, which each of us must face alone and independently in our effort to make a contribution to the whole. The setting sun symbolizes the end of an era, which inspires us to act in a timely manner and with a seriousness of purpose. The female warrior symbolizes the feminine creative force, who conceives in order to nurture and sustain that which is valuable. By pouring water on the desert sand, she actively encourages the growth of those seeds still hidden underground. The blue speech glyphs of her song symbolize the ritual meaning her everyday actions acquire in her moment-to-moment effort to unleash something new and wondrous upon the world. Taken together, these symbols represent the unified and integrated nature of the feminine half of the spirit warrior. That the water is drawn with jade beads and conch shells means that you recognize and revere the precious nature of that which evokes and sustains life. The full-grown maguey cactus symbolizes the success of past efforts to make hidden seeds sprout. Taken together, these symbols mean that you find a seed invisible to others that can thrive in even the most difficult conditions.

ACTION | The feminine half of the spirit warrior creates new possibilities for success. Because present circumstances are neither as fulfilling nor as secure as they once were, this is a time for actively planting the seeds of a smooth transition into more rewarding and dependable circumstances. As it is impossible at this stage to know which of your actions will ultimately bear fruit, it is necessary to make overtures in every arena in which you might conceivably be well-received. By daring to nurture the undeveloped potential inherent to every situation, you break not only your own expectations but those of others and, even though your actions might appear to lack conscious planning or purpose, they actually set the stage for your next endeavor. Look at your strengths and capabilities with new eyes, daring to imagine how different opportunities might nurture your own hidden potential. Explore new kinds of relationships, daring to imagine how different people might draw out parts of yourself you have not yet discovered. Because you seek success in order to bring *benefit* to the whole, you are aided by unseen forces whose sole intent is to bring you closer to your destiny.

INTENT | Before things actually come to an end, we still have the foundation from which to build a bridge to the next beginning. Rather than pursuing a single course of action, however, this is a time for opening as many doors and exploring as many roads as possible. Rather than basing decisions on precedents and past experience, watch for coincidences to emerge that inspire you to make decisions in a manner that surprises you. Before things actually begin anew, we still have the time to fully integrate the lessons of the past. Rather than leaping too quickly into the most comfortable circumstance, therefore, this is a time for becoming stronger and more content in and of yourself. Rather than succumbing to an unrealistic nostalgia for the past, risk exploring numerous detours even if they do not appear to lead to your future. Nurture the undeveloped potential you find wherever you are and your own development continues forever unabated.

SUMMARY | Pay attention to details others ignore. Take an interest in things others think beneath them. Take every possibility seriously, no matter how remote it seems. Leave no stone unturned in your search for the best road forward. Look at every chance to benefit others as an opportunity to hone your skills and increase your capabilities. Every act of generosity is a seed that eventually bears fruit.

The Line Changes

1ST When the body is not held sacred, it is mistreated and held in contempt—when nature is not held sacred, it is injured and held in contempt. As an individual, care for your body as if it were a noble being facing death. As a member of society, care for nature as if it were the visible half of spirit.

2ND When loved ones are not held sacred, they live and die without being seen—when humanity is not held sacred, it turns on itself with tooth and claw. As an individual, treat every loved one like a miracle. As a member of society, do not allow divide-and-conquer tactics to work.

3RD When learning is not held sacred, people can be herded like sheep—when qualified people are not held sacred, corrupt people rise to the top. As an individual, fulfill your infinite potential. As a member of society, do not reward power mongers and dilettantes with any say over your life.

4TH When creativity is not held sacred, people only know how to destroy—when creative people are not held sacred, the only kind of change people know is decay. As an individual, reunite the inner and outer worlds. As a member of society, upset stagnant balance so dynamic balance can be restored.

5TH When ethical conduct is held sacred, people correct their own faults—when ethical leaders are held sacred, the whole world trusts their fairness. As an individual, keep one foot on the pivot point of dignity at all times. As a member of society, treat everyone like your beloved grandmother.

6TH When wisdom is held sacred, people benefit by benefiting the whole—when wise leaders are held sacred, the whole world trusts their vision. As an individual, pool resources and share responsibilities. As a member of society, evoke peace and prospering for all.

CHANGING
ALLIANCES

IMAGE | A male warrior waves farewell to two warriors, one male and the other female, who wave back. He sets out on a road in the form of a serpent whose tongue touches a welcoming hand at the road's end. The warrior carries all he needs for a long and arduous journey. The place he leaves is lush with life, whereas his destination lies beyond a wilderness of deserts and mountains.

INTERPRETATION | This hexagram depicts the delicate transition facing those who leave behind one alliance to embark on another. The male warrior symbolizes the disciplined and honorable course of action. The male and female warriors he leaves behind symbolize an individual or group whose vision you no longer share. The way the three warriors wave to each other symbolizes a friendly leave-taking that is without rancor or enmity. That the road is in the form of a serpent means that you do not lose your way, no matter how the road might twist and turn. The serpent's tongue symbolizes a sense beyond our five senses, which allows us to find our way through life in a direct and intuitive manner. That the serpent's tongue touches the hand raised in greeting on the horizon means that you rely on your spirit guide to lead you to a new alliance that brings *benefit* to all concerned. That the warrior carries all he needs means that your past experience and training have prepared you to undertake this journey. That the place he leaves is lush with life, while his destination lies beyond a wilderness of deserts and mountains, means that you depart the known and familiar for the unknown and unforeseeable. Taken together, these symbols mean that you complete the journey from one alliance to another without weakening yourself or making new enemies.

ACTION | The masculine half of the spirit warrior tempers determination with compassion, sincerity with tact, and movement with grace. Once we find we are no longer compatible with our allies, it is necessary to disentangle ourselves from those allegiances in order to align ourselves with others whose values and actions are in harmony with our own. But if we merely act in a straightforward manner, with no concern for the future of those who have played an important part in our past, then we act decisively but without compassion: In the end, this creates resentments that come back to haunt us in our later endeavors. Similarly, integrity and truthfulness must fill our hearts when making dramatic changes in our lives but our words and actions do not belong solely to ourselves: Once we speak and act, we influence others and, if we are not careful and diplomatic outwardly, we find that many of our problems repeat themselves in our new endeavor. In the same way, even though our actions must be timely and sustain a certain momentum, we cannot afford to act clumsily or rudely or impatiently. If we do not cultivate and display poise, grace, and dignity when people are most easily offended, then we enter our next alliance with a proven inability to handle tense and distressing times without becoming unnerved ourselves. For these reasons, it is essential that you maintain a continuity of values in the midst of change, diligently discharging all your responsibilities before moving on to your next relationship. Because you steep yourself in the desire to be part of a more meaningful unity, your actions lead you to a period of more promising camaraderie, collaboration, and creativity.

INTENT | Good endings beget good beginnings. What is easy is starting new relationships, what is difficult is fulfilling them. What is easy is being at our best for a short time with people who do not know us well, what is difficult is being at our best for a long time with people who have come to know us well over a period of years. Most difficult of all is being at our best when we are bringing a long-standing relationship to a close. It is here we must be careful, paying attention to the details of our departure rather than allowing ourselves to be consumed by the adventure that awaits.

SUMMARY | Move patiently, be practical. Take the time to tie up loose ends, make the effort to ensure that those you leave behind feel strong and secure. Wherever there is a question of inequality or unfairness, it is best to take the loss upon yourself: People do not contest the outcome when they feel victorious. Act with dignity and honor. This change brings your way of life into greater harmony with your life's purpose.

THE LINE CHANGES

1ST When people have little experience, they use a naive form of imagination to fill in the gaps in what they know. This is merely jumping to conclusions and has nothing to do with understanding others. Cultivate friendships with people who live, think, believe, and act differently than you.

2ND When people form deep and lasting bonds, it is because they see past appearances and into the dreaming part of each other. This mirroring gaze, where dream and dream recognize one another, is a direct experience of the universality of essence. Open the door wider and all come into view.

3RD Roles and responsibilities have to be assigned based on the kind of understanding each possesses. Failure to do this places people in jarring and confusing circumstances. Contentment is more successful than success, so it may be more successful to step back than to step forward.

4TH Whom the leaders favor demonstrates whom they serve and permits you to know their values and ethics. Your own actions demonstrate whom you serve and permit you to know your own values and ethics. When your values and ethics differ from the leaders', do not abandon those you serve.

5TH To know your demeanor in the world, watch others' nonverbal response to your presence. To know your relevance in their lives, watch others' response to what you say in their presence. To know your influence on the lives of those nearby, watch how they have changed over time.

6TH When people have much experience, they should set limits on how much self-examination they engage in. Understanding should be directed outward instead, focusing on ways to improve conditions for people and nature. Use the wisdom you have gleaned from life to improve life.

STRENGTHENING
INTEGRITY

IMAGE | A female warrior and a male warrior are seated on a woven reed mat. Behind them, the sun hangs suspended above a great pyramid. Their bearing and clothing show that they are people of great dignity and merit. They are jointly seeking advice from the creators and ancestors by consulting the divinatory instrument drawn on the ground before them.

INTERPRETATION | This hexagram depicts the way for allies to strengthen the warrior's spirit in one another. The union of the female warrior and the male warrior symbolizes an alliance between individuals whose natures are complementary and mutually reinforcing. That they are seated together on the woven mat indicates that their alliance is based on a shared vision. That they are seated in front of the sunlit pyramid means that they acknowledge that they are descendants of great warriors who have gone on to live forever in the house of the sun. That they comport themselves as people of great dignity and merit means that they dedicate their lives to making both their ancestors and descendants proud. That they seek advice from the creators and the ancestors by consulting the divinatory instrument before them means that they honor and fulfill the ancient covenant between the visible and the invisible. Taken together, these symbols mean that you align yourself with others in order to transform your weaknesses into strengths.

ACTION | The masculine and feminine halves of the spirit warrior vigilantly treat one another with the respect, courtesy, and authenticity accorded great warriors. The skills and the knowledge of the old ways are of little value if they are not applied to present-day circumstances. In this sense, spirit warriors create relationships with one another in order to train themselves to live a balanced and harmonious way of life with the utmost integrity. As in every relationship, there are those who lead and those who follow—but among spirit warriors, these roles are extremely fluid and change constantly. One takes decisive action and another goes along, providing the utmost support. One moves in an indirect manner to increase harmony and good will, and another gives up the need for identifiable goals and concrete solutions. One challenges and another nourishes. One opens to new experiences and another gives up the need to control change. One takes on the role of the masculine half, another the role of the feminine half. One takes on the role of the feminine half, another the role of the masculine half. Back and forth, exchanging roles constantly, such allies face circumstances as a united front. Moving along with things when appropriate, creating resistance to things when appropriate, they use circumstances to train themselves to apply the old ways with honor, sincerity, and integrity. Because you make yourself such an ally, you find such allies and bring great *benefit* to all.

INTENT | What is difficult is to live the life of a spirit warrior all alone. Without relationships that support our goals, reinforce our values, and provide us complementary companionship, it is easy to give up our vision and accept a less demanding way of life. If we look around us for examples of how to live, we are sure to be drawn into a materialistic and self-centered way of life since other spirit warriors do not shout their presence. If we merely aim to conform to our surroundings, we are sure to drift into the orbit of something or someone seeking to use us for their own purposes. If, however, we align ourselves with allies striving to sustain the continuity of the old ones' vision of a balanced and harmonious way of life, we are sure to live the life of a noble and immortal spirit who has entered this realm in order to advance the great work of universal metamorphosis.

SUMMARY | Treat everyone as if they have a wise and immortal teacher within—and see everything they do as the teacher's subtle strategy for testing the depth of your perceptions. Treat everyone with respectful intimacy, avoid informal familiarity. Treat everyone like a great warrior armed with spear and shield—don't try to read others' minds. The relationships you cultivate now will endure forever.

THE LINE CHANGES

1ST   Insincerity abounds and people use one another without con-
       science, insecurity abounds and people take offense without
       giving others the benefit of the doubt. Make yourself the kind
       of person you want for a lifelong friend. Act from the heart and
       new allies will find you.

2ND   A strong relationship has many ups and downs over the course of
       its life and many people leave as soon as difficulties begin, hop-
       ing to find something more perfect. Steadfastness means holding
       together against tide and time. If you don't grow old together, you
       grow old alone.

3RD   Your reputation will suffer if you continue siding with this fac-
       tion and your hopes for advancement will not come to pass.
       When the choice is between imperfect but sincere superiors and
       passionate but opportunistic peers, you must choose the former.
       Make a clean break right away.

4TH   You have the skills needed to advance the goals of those above—
       place yourself in their service and they will further your own
       goals. These are honorable souls who can be trusted to treat all
       in a beneficial manner. Learn from them that truly successful
       people do not speak of success.

5TH   Success isolates people, making them suspicious of others'
       motives and protective of their real thoughts. Reach across the
       social spectrum to keep your heart young, your spirit laughing,
       and to make friends from all walks of life. Learn from them that
       intimidation just strengthens your enemy.

6TH   The leadership of this group is not living the kind of life they
       are espousing. Look through the talk and posturing and you
       will find empty costumes. Truly beneficial people do not act like
       this—they are open, straightforward, and plain spoken. You have
       nothing to learn from these people.

CONCEIVING
SPIRIT

IMAGE | A male warrior receives a vision of a great feathered serpent whose inner nature is a roaring jaguar.

INTERPRETATION | The male warrior symbolizes the versatility and fortitude of the disciplined spirit. That he receives a vision means that your ability to sense the invisible grows stronger. The feathered serpent symbolizes the divine twin, the higher self, the light of wisdom and understanding. That the feathered serpent's inner nature is a roaring jaguar means that within even the most subtle and profound understanding, an even more subtle and profound mystery demands to be heard. Taken together, these symbols mean that you grow stronger and more resourceful by attuning your senses to the world of spirit right before your eyes.

ACTION | The masculine half of the spirit warrior breaks through the barrier separating matter and spirit. Such a barrier is erected in our minds by the constant training we receive from those who find advantage in promoting the separation of people from nature, from each other, and from their own true self. If people everywhere perceived matter and spirit to be the same thing, after all, the ignorance, cruelty, and suffering that make up much of human history would end. If we were all to experience the material form of nature as spirit, we would stop harming it by diminishing it faster than we help it replenish itself. If we were all to experience the material form of people everywhere as spirit, we would stop harming one another by acting as if our own rights and desires are superior to those of others. If we were all to experience the material form of our own individual bodies as spirit, we would stop harming ourselves by doubting that every thought, feeling, and action play a pivotal role in eternity. Breaking through such a mental barrier is a matter of constant training, as well: If we do not use every thought, feeling, and action to intensify our experience of matter as spirit, we continue to desecrate the temple of nature, the temple of civilization, and the temple of individuality. Because you increasingly see the invisible within the visible, your thoughts are filled with insight, your feelings with good will, and your actions with *benefit.*

INTENT | When the warrior's spirit has become second nature, we inevitably come to see through the foremost artifice of the enemy-within. A rigorous cultivation of the warrior's spirit is, in effect, a prolonged act of laying siege to the stronghold of the enemy-within: True victory is achieved only when the walls have been broken and the hostage set free. In this sense, the hostage is our innate awareness of the oneness of all things, the walls of the stronghold are the views of separateness we have been trained to accept as real, and the enemy-within is the traitor who takes hostage the true heir and usurps the throne of experience. By reminding ourselves constantly that the present boundaries of our awareness do not mark the furthest limits of awareness, we strip away all the false views that have accrued to the lower self over the course of this lifetime. In this way, we clear our eyes of the cobwebs that have obstructed our seeing the world of spirit right before our eyes.

SUMMARY | A momentous change is at hand. All your life the soul has looked at the world through your eyes but now you are beginning to look at the world through the soul's eyes. Everything you undertake will benefit others and make you a treasured part of your relationships. Treat everything with the reverence due an aspect of the divine. Leave behind worry, trust that your path is blessed.

THE LINE CHANGES

1ST It is the season to congregate and enjoy being with others by attending public spectacles in the arts, sciences, and athletics. It is the season to congregate in celebration of traditional religious and political holidays. Shared physical experiences fuse people into a cohesive whole.

2ND Honoring everyone but your own extended family reveals the blind spot of ingratitude. Honoring no one but your own extended family reveals the blind spot of insecurity. Honoring all as your extended family reveals the clear-slightness of good will—be ever more inclusive in your heart.

3RD Selfishness is the enemy-within—in the midst of much personal evolution, you are surprised to find a nagging resentment toward the needs of others. This is the aspect of sharing that puts your ideals to the test. If you don't force things, you will prove to yourself that benefiting others benefits you.

4TH There are people who will use your enthusiasm, idealism, and talents to advance their own cause. If you find yourself taking advantage of others' hopes and fears, then you have been duped into doing your superiors' dirty work for them. Quit and go forward.

5TH The bond between above and below is unbreakable, forged in the fires of many shared trials and tribulations. You can count on this relationship to the end—just as the union of man and woman produces a child, you are producing something that will outlast you. Radiate the peace you feel.

6TH In the final analysis, there are things that cannot be shared with others—mysteries, paradoxes, inexpressible longings, impossible visions. Such is the fate of every individual—it is the well, in fact, of what makes us individual. Continue your quest for absolute at-one-ment.

AWAKENING
SELF-SUFFICIENCY

IMAGE | A great feathered serpent hatches out of the earth as if from an egg. Its feathers are adorned with conch shells and it senses its surroundings with its bifurcated tongue.

INTERPRETATION | This hexagram represents the great forces released by the accumulated efforts of spirit warriors over the ages. The feathered serpent symbolizes the collective intent and vision shared by spirit warriors in every time and every place. That it hatches from the earth as if from an egg means that the community of spirit incubating within the material world emerges as a living, dynamic force of creation. The conches adorning its feathers symbolize the call for all to join the community of spirit. Its bifurcated tongue symbolizes the duality that is one. That it uses its bifurcated tongue to sense its surroundings means that you are attuned to the universal presence of the masculine and feminine creative forces. Taken together, these symbols mean that you align yourself with those whose only *need* is to bring *benefit* to their surroundings.

ACTION | The spirit warrior reverses the flow of power, channeling it inside instead of outside. By storing up power internally rather than expending it externally, we are able to both free ourselves of habits and gain control over our actions. This inner autonomy also extricates us from social influences that strive to mold us into obedient marionettes even as it allows us to be more tolerant of the deeper motives of those social influences. From the spirit warrior's perspective, the original intent of religion is to awaken the higher soul to its potential freedom while purifying the lower soul of fear, greed, envy, and hate—just as the original intent of government is to awaken the higher soul to its responsibility to others while instilling in the lower soul the capacity for self-control. From this perspective, the fact that religion and government acquire ulterior motives over time and begin to act in their own self-interest merely demonstrates that they are managed by human beings and must be viewed accordingly. Similarly, the fact that all religions and governments strive to awaken the higher soul and purify the lower soul—even when they have forgotten how and why—simply demonstrates that the quest for metamorphosis is a universal and irresistible force. In other words, just as our inner autonomy releases us from the trap of depending on social influences for our sense of self, it also releases us from the trap of not seeing how those social influences contribute, however unintentionally, to the gradual unification of humanity. Reversing the flow of power, we gain inner autonomy and, paradoxically, become one with the universal civilizing force.

INTENT | The wise become independent even from what they revere. Like children who are grown up and independent of the parents they love and admire, spirit warriors take their place among the community of spiritual equals. Because you use this lifetime to bring the most *benefit* to others, you incubate the higher soul that is preparing to hatch from the lower soul: Joining in the collective labor shared by spirit warriors in every time and every place, you contribute directly to both the fulfillment of humanity's destiny and the creator's vision. Becoming part of the universal civilizing spirit, you contribute directly to the founding of a free and harmonious world of equals right here within this world.

SUMMARY | Only the body marks the passage of time—for the soul, there is only this everlasting moment of growing. Let five rivers of energy come in through the senses, let them run together into a sea of growing power. Do not expend it on petty thoughts, moods, or goals. Send forth your rain clouds only to water the valuable. Condense intent into actions that foster peace and prosperity for all. Your success is inevitable.

THE LINE CHANGES

1ST   You look for a shortcut but do not find one—you would like to make the journey in a single step. This is admirable but not in your control—move according to the advice you are given. Even those who find the shortcut must spend the same amount of time refining their character.

2ND   It is difficult to find a lifelong ally who will aid you on your journey and treat you like a long-lost companion. If you have found such a person, give them all your trust and respect. If you have not, keep your eyes and mind and heart open—make yourself worthy of attracting such a benefactor.

3RD   The higher must not desert the lower, although it does not concur with many of its actions. The lower must nourish the higher, although it finds it often unrealistic. Fuse the two into a viable whole and they will be able to ward off every kind of destruction.

4TH   Not all partnerships are self-evident at first—the strong may act weak, the flexible may act rigid. One nearby will make a good partner—look closer at those around you and peer beneath surface appearances. The right one may be ignoring you because you too are not acting like your true self.

5TH   The window of opportunity opens—higher and lower recognize one another and reunite as if no time had passed. Such profound feelings of timeless affection cannot arise in strangers' hearts—it is no secret that halves are fated to rejoin. Be unsparing in your support and devotion.

6TH   In the midst of the marketplace, you are alone and undisturbed. The years have gone by and altered you in their passing. What you were unable to achieve all at once by sheer force of will has been accomplished without your noticing it—keep polishing until it is time to do something else.

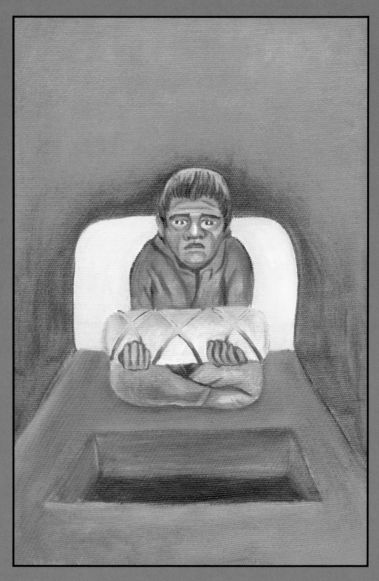

SAFEGUARDING
LIFE

IMAGE | A male warrior holds the funeral bundle of his child, preparing to place it in its burial site. His face reflects the shock, anguish, and horror that fills his heart.

INTERPRETATION | This hexagram depicts the inevitable result of carelessness and irreverence. The male warrior symbolizes the versatility and fortitude that are at the core of outer nurturing. That he prepares to place the funeral bundle of his child in its burial site means that strength cannot accomplish afterwards what nurturing can accomplish beforehand. That his face and heart are filled with shock, anguish, and horror means that he is in the grips of the most terrible truth: That which we most cherish cannot be replaced. Taken together, these symbols mean that you avoid causing suffering by honoring and nurturing all that your spirit touches.

ACTION | The masculine half of the spirit warrior draws back from the brink before it is too late. It is not a time for pursuing desires and ambitions. Those who cannot temper their strength run the risk of losing a source of that strength. When our masculine half goes too far in pursuit of goals and becomes short-sighted and impatient, it is necessary to balance it with the strongest medicine possible: Real problems can be avoided only by balancing the masculine half with the power of the feminine half's protective love. It is the feminine half's sense of caring and reverence that holds the key to fulfilling the real goal of happiness, companionship, and a clear conscience. Those who do not hold the emotions of caring and reverence dear to their hearts run the risk of causing pain for themselves and others. Just because we can acquire something doesn't mean we should; just because we can accomplish something doesn't mean we have to. Stopping to really consider what we are risking, allowing ourselves to feel the full brunt of such an emotional loss—this is the protective and loving nature of the feminine half's medicine. Likewise, stubborn pursuit of goals even in the face of warning signs, longing for something that threatens to cause suffering for others, refusal to change course when it endangers the greater good—this is the short-sighted and zealous nature of the masculine half when it loses its balance and sense of proportion. Because you treat nature, other people, and your own creations with the care and reverence you would your own infant child, you counteract every self-defeating action before it ever arises in thought or feeling.

INTENT | The foolish ruin even that upon which they depend. When we recognize the sanctity of life, however, and work to protect it from unnecessary and pointless harm, then we safeguard our own spiritual foundation and that of all who touch our spirit. Consider what cannot be replaced and then cherish it, planting seeds of intent in the spirit realm to nurture it and keep it from being lost forever. Shun materialism and self-interest as you would a poisoned well. Keep to the path of the balanced and harmonious way of life, revering all that the life-giving and life-sustaining forces themselves love. By maintaining an unbroken alliance with the helping spirits, the community of spirit warriors ensures that the hidden storehouse of life-giving power is never depleted. Only in this way can human nature continue to draw upon the power to create its own, unforeseeable, future.

SUMMARY | If you lose sight of your dreams, you will lose what you have already won. If you become self-absorbed and self-indulgent, you will lose your way. Recognize the crossroads when you come to them: Will you take the way of self-gratification and self-glorification or the way of balance and harmony? Profound success is yours if you can reverse the momentum before it is too late.

THE LINE CHANGES

1ST Your predecessors have left the family home a mess—brothers, sisters, and cousins are all fighting for a bigger part of the inheritance. Clearing all this up is made harder by factions invested in perpetuating conflict. The utmost resolution and diplomacy will have to be applied for a long time.

2ND The primal relationship between humans and nature has been disrupted by your predecessors' short-sightedness. Look upon nature as you would your beloved and work to repair this rift. Begin by puncturing the bubble alienating you from the affection surrounding you.

3RD Poverty, crime, and desperation are a way of life for many as the loss of meaningful employment takes its toll. Look deeper into the dehumanizing effect of technology and materialism. Participate actively in a long-range strategy to bring the collective mind and collective heart back into harmony.

4TH It would be ideal if simply admitting the wrong-doing of your predecessors were enough to rectify their mistakes. But such is not the case—you still have much work ahead of you. Only by persevering in benefiting those around you can the old order be overthrown from within.

5TH You have made a good start but do not really have the stomach for some of the difficult decisions ahead. Find someone trustworthy to enact reforms. Focus on encouraging people to advance by reminding them of the positive accomplishments of their predecessors that will remain in place.

6TH Seeing how corruption worms its way back in even as reforms are being implemented, you know the time has come to leave and take up the greater pursuits of life. Break your habit of looking for what needs reforming. Now is the time to look into the face of what is perfect in the world.

Toltec I Ching Number and Name		Hexagram	King Wen #	Toltec I Ching Number and Name		Hexagram	King Wen #
1	Provoking Change		51	17	Guiding Force		11
2	Sensing Creation		58	18	Resolving Paradox		64
3	Recognizing Ancestry		9	19	Celebrating Passage		45
4	Mirroring Wisdom		50	20	Entering Service		60
5	Restoring Wholeness		42	21	Cultivating Character		26
6	Fostering Self-Sacrifice		32	22	Sharing Memory		56
7	Compelling Motive		28	23	Wielding Passion		38
8	Harmonizing Duality		61	24	Revealing Knowledge		43
9	Uprooting Fear		3	25	Radiating Intent		34
10	Unifying Inspiration		16	26	Dignifying Ambition		21
11	Attracting Allies		17	27	Trusting Intuition		14
12	Seeing Ahead		54	28	Synchronizing Movement		7
13	Concentrating Attention		62	29	Sustaining Resilience		57
14	Unlocking Evolution		27	30	Transforming Extinction		52
15	Belonging Together		49	31	Embracing Noninterference		36
16	Renewing Devotion		10	32	Controlling Confrontation		6

Toltec I Ching Number and Name		Hexagram	King Wen #	Toltec I Ching Number and Name		Hexagram	King Wen #
33	Accepting Instruction		55	49	Staying Open		15
34	Evoking Opposite		25	50	Narrowing Aim		4
35	Holding Back		41	51	Living Essence		1
36	Stabilizing Communion		31	52	Growing Certainty		30
37	Penetrating Confusion		39	53	Mastering Reason		63
38	Dissolving Artifice		23	54	Repeating Test		12
39	Reviving Tradition		37	55	Internalizing Purity		33
40	Adapting Experience		44	56	Recapturing Vision		22
41	Feigning Compliance		35	57	Defying Uncertainty		29
42	Interpreting Insight		5	58	Dawning Existence		2
43	Going Beyond		24	59	Developing Potential		48
44	Refining Instinct		40	60	Changing Alliances		20
45	Casting Off		19	61	Strengthening Integrity		8
46	Honoring Contentment		47	62	Conceiving Spirit		13
47	Making Individual		46	63	Awakening Self-Sufficiency		53
48	Moving Source		59	64	Safeguarding Life		18

GLOSSARY

BENEFIT The natural, appropriate, and spontaneous response to *need*.

CIVILIZATION The single collective body manifesting the metamorphosing spirit of *humanity*.

COIN METHOD One of numerous methods used to consult the *Oracle*. Other methods include the traditional yarrow stalk method and modern use of computers' random number generators.

DIVINATION The art and practice of interpreting signs and symbols to see into the *essence* of things.

ENEMY-WITHIN The conditioned and artificial aspect of every individual's personality that is acquired unconsciously from their surroundings and must be consciously extinguished through *training* in order for each person to return to their essential nature. The set of self-defeating behaviors and perceptions that the *spirit warrior* defeats.

ESSENCE The living presence of the *One Spirit* manifesting itself in every creation at every moment. The unchanging background of all change that makes up the underlying harmony of all creation. The timeless perfection of all things underlying their apparent imperfection.

FEMININE CREATIVE FORCE The sustaining half of the *One Spirit*. The natural, appropriate, and spontaneous benevolence of all creation, whereby all things are accorded an equal measure of essential *benefit*. The universal principle of water, which nurtures all it touches and, within the individual, manifests as the feminine half of the *spirit warrior*.

HEXAGRAMS The 64 six-lined symbols of the *I Ching* by which the *Oracle* gives voice to the *One Spirit*. When the oracle's answer includes *line changes*, then the first hexagram describes the present situation and the second hexagram describes the future situation evolving out of existing trends.

HOUSE OF THE SUN A metaphor for the One Spirit, the origin and destination of all souls, the Home to which we all return after death. Great *spirit warriors* of the past come back from it in order to inspire and encourage the living.

HUMANITY The self-aware aspect of creation born from the union of *nature* and *spirit*. The single collective *spirit* of *civilization*, which must consciously defeat its own *enemy-within*.

I CHING The *Oracle* of the indigenous shamanic world view of ancient China, which became the repository of wisdom collected by the savants of that culture. It posits a single unifying presence, called the Tao, or The Way, which creates and sustains all things from within by means of the union of its Yang and Yin halves. The way in which the Yang and Yin creative forces alternate, much like the seasons, through the six dimensions of creation is mirrored in the six-lined *hexagrams* of the *oracle*. As a system of symbols representing the natural order of creation itself, it directly mirrors the pattern of perception inherent to *humanity*.

LINE CHANGES The turning points of transition between the present hexagram and future hexagram of the oracle, represented by the numbers 6, 7, 8, and 9. (In the I Ching divination method, the initial result of 6 is a changing yin line, 7 a stable yang line, 8 a stable yin line, and 9 a changing yang line.) As manifestations of the masculine and feminine creative forces, these numbers signify the manner by which the nature of the six lines change: A 7 represents Spring, which grows too hot as the 9 of Summer and turns into the 8 of Autumn, which grows too cold as the 6 of Winter and turns into the 7 of Spring.

MASCULINE CREATIVE FORCE The creating half of the *One Spirit*. The natural, appropriate, and spontaneous catalyst of all creation, whereby all things are inspired to take form and strive toward continual *metamorphosis*. The universal principle of fire, which ignites all it touches and, within the individual, manifests as the masculine half of the *spirit warrior*.

METAMORPHOSIS The natural, appropriate, and spontaneous return to *essence*, understood as the result of self-liberation, which does not imply liberating the self but, rather, that liberation can only be achieved by oneself.

NATURE The visible half of *spirit*. The single body of the *One Spirit*. The living and aware form of the sacred.

NEED A temporary blockage in the free flow of *benefit* among all things.

NEW WORLD The Golden Age of Humanity, marked by universal peace and prospering, that is arising out of the ashes of the old world of conflict and greed. The emerging Classic Period of *civilization*, in which every culture is created equal, society exists to afford every individual every opportunity to fulfill their potential, and every individual voluntarily fulfills their responsibility to conscientiously contribute to the Golden Age of Humanity.

ONE SPIRIT The single immaterial living awareness of the material universe. The origin and destination of every individual *soul* and, thereby, the eternal repository of all the memories and experiences of all who have ever lived. The marriage of the *masculine creative force* and the *feminine creative force*, whose union of Light and Love creates and sustains all of creation.

ORACLE The means by which the *One Spirit* gives voice to the *essence* of situations and the trends developing out of them. The natural, appropriate, and spontaneous response of the *One Spirit* to an individual's act of *divination*.

SOUL The personal aspect of *spirit*.

SPIRIT The invisible half of *nature*. The living awareness within all matter.

SPIRIT GUIDE Personal aspects of the *One Spirit* that instruct and guide the living. Also called ancestors, guardian spirit, companion spirit, spiritual ally, spiritual twin, unseen forces, etc., because they are experienced as benevolent souls still dedicated to the founding of the Golden Age of Humanity.

SPIRIT WARRIOR A man or woman engaged in consciously defeating the *enemy-within*. Women or men consciously training themselves to unite their feminine and masculine halves in order to promote and share in the good fortune of all.

TOLTEC The indigenous shamanic world view of ancient Mexico that influenced all those who followed because of its ideal of a civilization in which art, science, and spirituality are one and the same. It posits a single unifying presence which creates and sustains all things by means of the union of the *masculine creative force* and the *feminine creative force*. The way in which these two forces manifest is mirrored in the six compass points of East, West, North, South, Center, and Above. A spiritual lineage of savants who continue to return from the Home of the One Spirit in order to inspire and encourage the living.

TONALPOALLI The divinatory calendar of ancient Mexico whose 260 days result from all the possible combinations of its 20 daysigns and 13 numerical co-efficients. Held sacred because every 104 cycles of the solar year of 365 days (37,960 days) equals 65 cycles of the Venus year of 584 days (37,960 days) and 146 cycles of the divinatory calendar of 260 days (37,960 days). Beyond this, the 780-day year of Mars is precisely three cycles of the 260-day calendar. It is also hypothesized that it is held sacred because approximately 260 days pass between the time a woman realizes she is pregnant and the birth of her child. People in various ancient cultures (the Mixtecs, for example) had both a personal name and a calendrical name, which was based on the day of their birth. The divinatory nature of the *Tonalpoalli* is exemplified in various indigenous manuscripts, especially the Borgia Codex.

TRAINING Consciously working to eradicate the thinking errors based on self-interest by concentrating on thoughts and feelings based on good will toward all. Consciously working to quiet the inner monolog and experience each moment of life just as it is, without interpreting it in reference to oneself.

TRIGRAM The three-lined symbols of the *I Ching*, whose possible combinations result in its 64 *hexagrams*. As analogs of naturally occurring states of change, the combinations of inner and outer trigrams generate the 64 essential situations in which all entities, whether individual or collective, find themselves at any given time.

UNIVERSAL CIVILIZING SPIRIT The innate sense of rightness and fairness inherent to humanity since time immemorial, which works from within to create a civilization based on justice and humaneness.

INDEX

CHART OF TRIGRAMS AND HEXAGRAMS

	Upper Trigram							
Lower Trigram	2	23	8	45	16	12	20	35
	15	52	39	31	62	33	53	56
	7	4	29	47	40	6	59	64
	19	41	60	58	54	10	61	38
	24	27	3	17	51	25	42	21
	11	26	5	43	34	1	9	14
	46	18	48	28	32	44	57	50
	36	22	63	49	55	13	37	30

Locate your hexagram number at the point where its upper and lower trigrams intersect.

GLOBAL *community*
INDIVIDUAL *awakening*

Larson Publications
larsonpublications.com

Larson Publications aspires to help bring forward a
new, creative universal outlook that embraces and transcends divisions
of east and west, north and south, believers and nonbelievers.